CW00971985

BROWNIE COOK-BOOK

VERILY ANDERSON

Brownie cook-book

Illustrated by Ted Draper

BROCKHAMPTON PRESS

ISBN 0 340 10437 6

First edition 1972
Second impression 1973
Published by Brockhampton Press Ltd, Salisbury Road, Leicester
Printed in Great Britain by Butler & Tanner Ltd, Frome

Contents

1 · *Hello cooks!*

Every time you cook you will need:

(1) Your hands, newly washed each time. Fingers are often more useful than forks and spoons and knives in cooking. You can bend them and wiggle them to get into odd corners and they can do more delicate things. So don't be afraid to use them if it's easier. Food feels good as well as tasting and looking and smelling good. Only don't forget to wash your hands in between handling different kinds of food.

(2) Clean apron.

(3) Ribbon or hair grip to keep your hair and the food out of each other. Chefs wear white caps and you could too.

Each different thing you cook has a list of its own of the FOOD you have to collect before you begin and another list of the TOOLS you will need to cook with. The list of different foods and the way to cook them is called a RECIPE (only you call it a *ressippy* when you say it out loud).

The recipes here are arranged in stages. Read the

recipe right through to see if it looks like the kind of thing you would like to cook. When you have chosen what you are going to cook, read the FOOD list right through to see what you need for it.

You may have to ask Mummy to buy some of the things on the list next time she goes shopping. Perhaps she will let you go and buy them yourself.

TOOLS

Read the TOOLS list right through before you begin and make sure you know what each tool is for. Some tools have several names so match up your tools with names used in this book.

If you see ounces and pounds in the food list, you know you will need a weighing machine.

Knife. Any knife that will cut. Kitchen knives with a point are sometimes too sharp to be safe. You are better off with a table knife, or use any light fork.

Use a *wooden spoon* when the recipe says so. *Metal spoons* get too hot if you use them for stirring and the tips get worn away.

Bowl. Any bowl or basin big enough to do the job needed.

Wooden board for chopping and rolling and handling sticky things on.

Pastry cutter for stamping out pastry and cake shapes. Choose the shape and size you need.

Thimble is not really a kitchen tool except for stamping out very small biscuits.

Frying pan for cooking food fast in a little fat.

Saucepan for boiling and stewing in water and for making sauces in.

Slice for scooping up eggs, fish, etc., from a frying pan.

Sieve for sifting flour and straining soup through.

Colander: bigger and stronger with fewer, bigger holes, for straining and steaming rice and vegetables.

Egg whisk for beating air into eggs and cream to make them grow thicker and more.

Rolling pin. Not really a pin at all. For rolling out pastry or heavily crushing baked crusts to make crumbs.

Lemon squeezer and *cheese grater* do what they say.

Wire rack for airing cakes and buns after they come out of the oven.

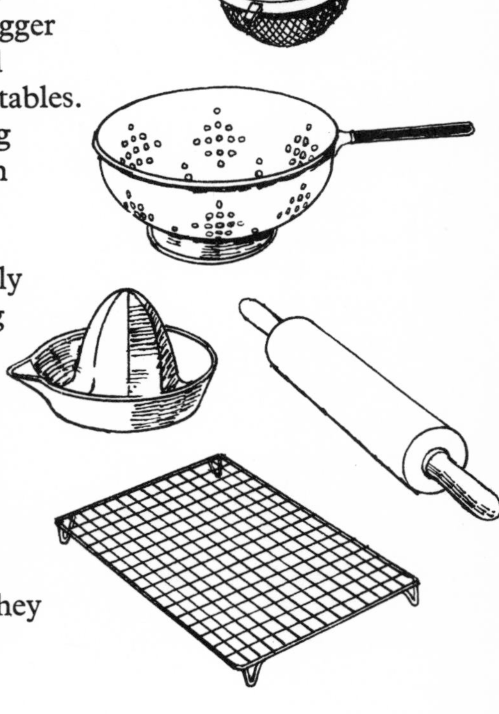

A *measuring jug* is marked inside, usually up to one pint. Pour milk or water in up to the mark you need.

Cake tin. Round tin for baking cakes in, sometimes with a bottom that comes out.

Baking sheet. Tray for baking scones and some kinds of buns on.

Patty pan tin. Six, nine, or twelve little pans all joined together as one tin for baking buns and little cakes in.

Kitchen paper, or greaseproof, for lining baking tins.
Use a scrap of greaseproof paper rubbed in a little butter for greasing tins.

Tinfoil for wrapping food in to cook in the oven.

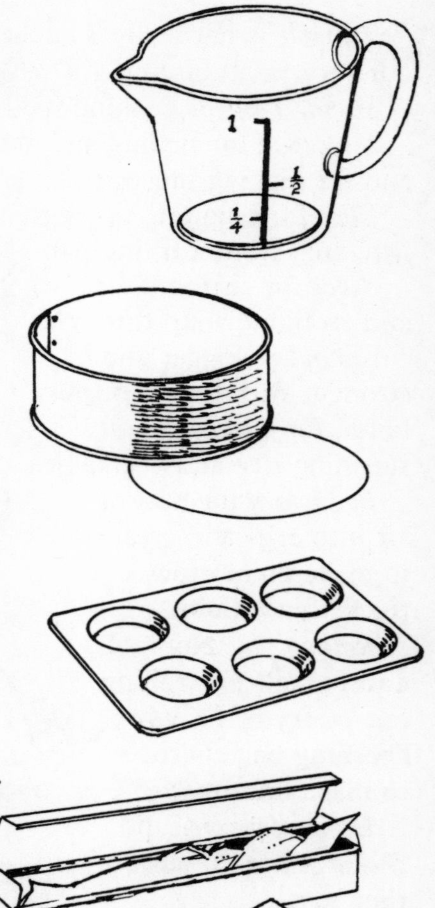

Skewer for pinning meat in place, testing cakes and making a drip.

Ramikin pot. Small ovenproof dish for baking single egg in.

Scissors for cutting paper and cardboard shapes. Useful, too, for cutting off bacon rinds and the pith from oranges and grapefruit; and for shaping their skin.

HEATING THE OVEN

Until you have cooked a lot with Mummy's help, ask her to put the oven on ten minutes before you need it. The numbers in the recipes show how hot it should be. The first number in brackets (Mark 3) is for gas ovens. The second number (325°) is for electric and other kinds.

When everything is ready, hands washed, apron on and hair tidied out of the way, put all the FOOD and all the TOOLS on the table.

Read the recipe right through again, looking at the pictures as you go, then follow it step by step.

TIDY AS MUCH AS YOU CAN AS YOU GO

If you rush at the cooking and forget about the tidying there may be a dreadful muddle at the end. When there's a lull, make the most of it. Put the saucepans in the sink and fill them up with cold water, stack the spoons and knives and forks in the water and later on you will be able to wash them up more easily. How ever well your cooking comes out, the job is not done till the kitchen is clean and neat and just how you found it.

BEGINNER Brownies begin here.
MIDDLING Brownies begin in the middle.
BIG Brownies begin where they like.

NO Brownies boil or bake or fry or roast without a grown-up to say they can!

Read through for fun, then try out anything you like the look of till you have one or two specials you can cook really well without looking at the book.

2 · *Teddy's tea party*

Have you ever made a party for Teddy? Everything has to be made very small to fit on a doll's tea-set.

The day Mummy makes pastry is a good one for a Teddy's tea. She's sure to have some scraps over already rolled out flat so you can cut them into any little shapes you like or make them into thimble biscuits.

FOOD
Scraps of uncooked pastry
½ cup flour
½ saucer of water

TOOLS
Thimble
Knife
Board
Baking sheet

1 Cut twelve strips of the pastry about as long as your little finger for the crosses.

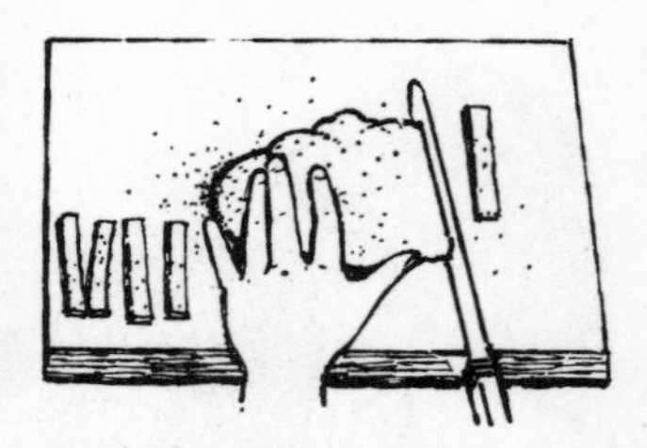

2 Lay one strip across another to make a cross and stick them together by dipping your finger in the water and dabbing it on the middle of the underneath strip.

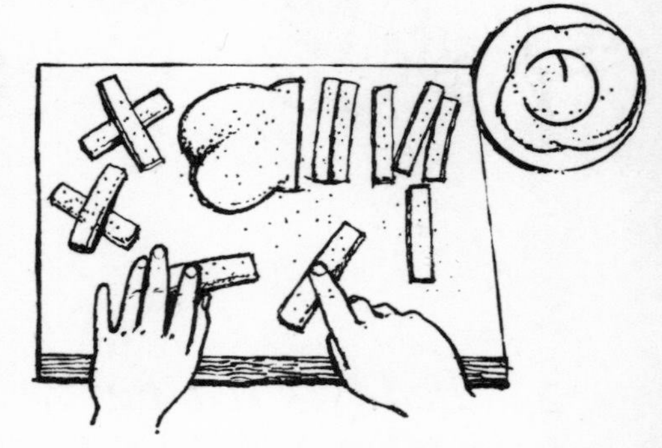

3 Dip the thimble in the flour and stamp out six rounds of pastry for the noughts. Make sure each one comes out of the thimble.

4 Shake a little flour on the baking tin and arrange the noughts and crosses on it, not touching.

Ask Mummy to bake them in the oven for about 7 minutes. (Mark 4 or 350°.)

Teddy's sandwiches need to be very small. Ask Mummy for:

FOOD
2 slices thin bread and butter
A spoonful of honey

TOOLS
Knife
Board

1 Spread one slice of bread and butter with honey and put the other slice over it, butter downwards. Press it down all over.

2 Cut the crusts off and then cut this big sandwich in half, corner to corner, and then in half again and then again so you have eight tiny little diagonal sandwiches.

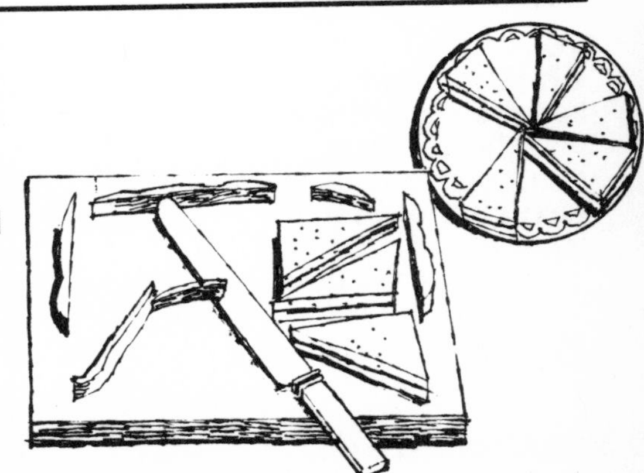

FOOD
2 thick slices of bread
2 oz. of butter
2 oz. of icing sugar
2 teaspoonfuls of drinking chocolate
2 oz. sweets or a candle.
(How old is Teddy?)

TOOLS
Knife
Board
Plate
Bowl
Large round pastry cutter
Wooden spoon

1 With the pastry cutter stamp out two rounds of bread.

Mix butter and sugar together with wooden spoon till they're creamy and stir in drinking chocolate to make **chocolate butter icing.**

2 Divide the butter icing in the bowl into three big blobs. Spread one blob on a round of bread and put the other round on to it but don't press it down.

3 Hold Teddy's cake between your finger and thumb in one hand and spread the next blob of butter icing round the sides.

Put the cake down to spread the last blob on the top.

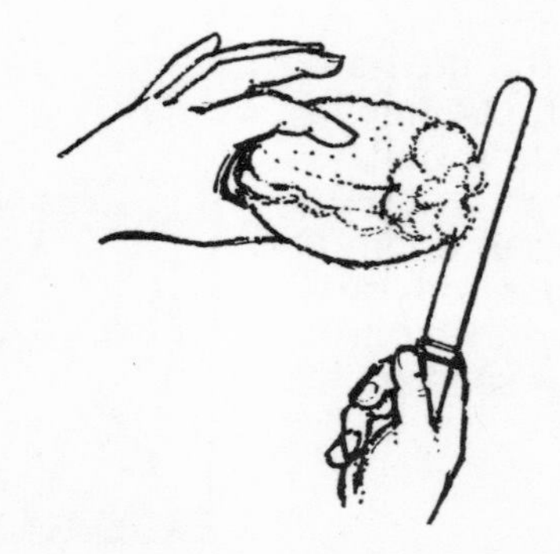

4 Put small sweets or hundreds-and-thousands on the top to look pretty. Make a T for Teddy out of a row of little sweets or two strips cut from a big one, or add the candle.

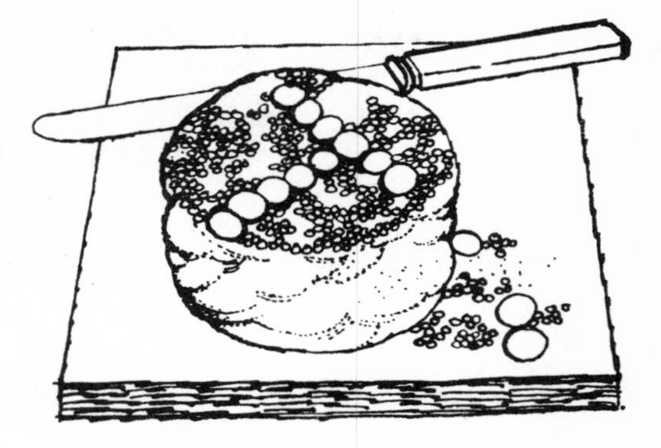

Put the birthday cake on the table and throw away all the crumbs and mess. Wipe the board clean and wash up the knife and bowls. Take off your apron, wash your hands and tidy your hair and Teddy's party is all ready to begin.

Bring him to the table and put him in the most important place. Offer him sandwiches and pour out drinks for you all. You and your friend can finish up anything Teddy doesn't eat. Help him to cut the birthday cake and don't forget to take a slice to Mummy.

When the party is over wash up the cups and saucers and start thinking about what you are going to cook next time.

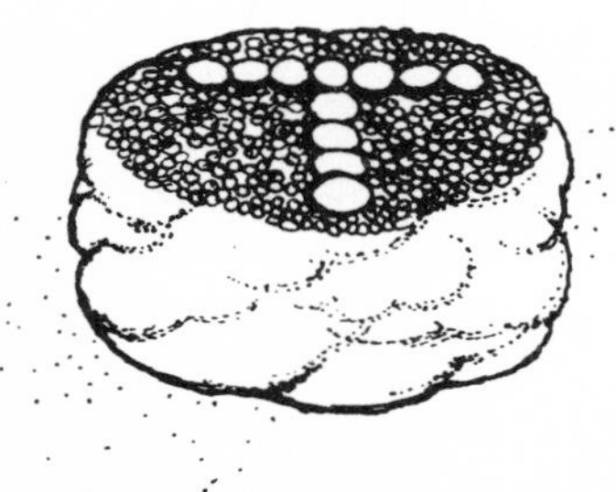

3 · *Helping Mummy*

A good Brownie helps her mother by getting things out for her and putting them away when she has finished, making sure, by asking, that she puts them in their usual places. If you put the cheese-grater away in the cat's cupboard, or the sugar on the saucepan shelf, Mummy would rather do it herself next time.

If Mummy is going to make a cake you can help by weighing the butter, sugar and flour. You can practise weighing other things too at the same time. It is very useful to know what certain things weigh in case you ever have to cook without a weighing machine.

Three level tablespoons of flour
weigh one ounce.

Four level tablespoonfuls of grated cheese
weigh one ounce.

Two level tablespoons of granulated or castor sugar
weigh one ounce.

Two and a half level tablespoonfuls of icing sugar
weigh one ounce.

One level tablespoonful of syrup or runny honey weighs one ounce.

A packet of butter, margarine or fat weighs eight ounces. Cut it in half for four ounces and in quarters for two ounces.

Next time Mummy makes

Weight-of-an-egg Buns or a Cake

you can help her by weighing all the food in eggs.

FOOD
2 Eggs
The weight of 2 eggs in flour
The weight of 2 eggs in butter
The weight of 2 eggs in sugar

For a bigger cake use more eggs and their weight in flour, butter and sugar.

And you can get out the TOOLS:

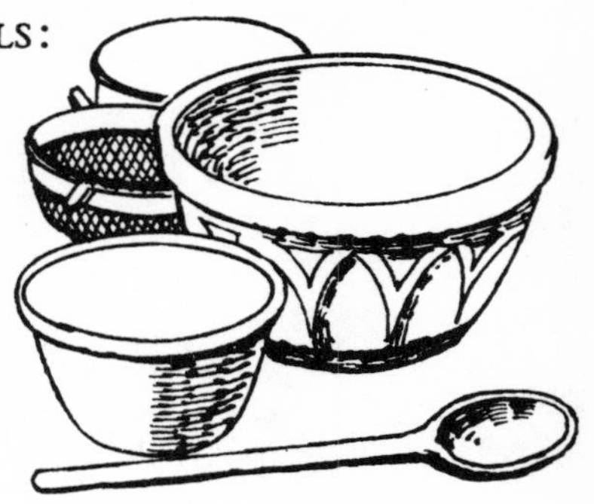

Big mixing bowl
Small bowl for
breaking eggs into
Wooden spoon for stirring
Fork for beating
Sieve for sifting the flour in
Patty pan tin or cake tin

And you can get the patty pan tin ready. Every time a cake (or buns) is baked it needs to have its inside rubbed all over with the paper the butter has been wrapped in, with a little butter left on. This prevents the cake from sticking to the tin.

Watch how Mummy:

1 Puts the butter and sugar in the bowl and goes on mixing them until they are creamy.

2 Breaks the eggs into the small bowl and beats them up together with the fork.

3 Slowly pours the eggs into the mixing bowl, and beats them all together.

4 Puts the flour into the sieve and shakes it lightly on to the mixture, then stirs it in.

5 Spoons the mixture into the patty pans.

6 Puts the tins in a medium oven (Mark 4, 350°) for about ten minutes.

While the buns are cooking you can make the icing.

FOOD
2 oz. butter
4 oz. icing sugar

TOOLS
Wooden spoon
Knife
Bowl
Skewer

1 Mix the butter and icing sugar together in the bowl till it's creamy, like Mummy did for the buns.

2 Cakes and buns are tested to see whether they are done with a skewer, which is pushed lightly in. If it comes out clean and shiny then they are ready to come out of the oven.

3 The middle of each bun will have risen up in a little bump.

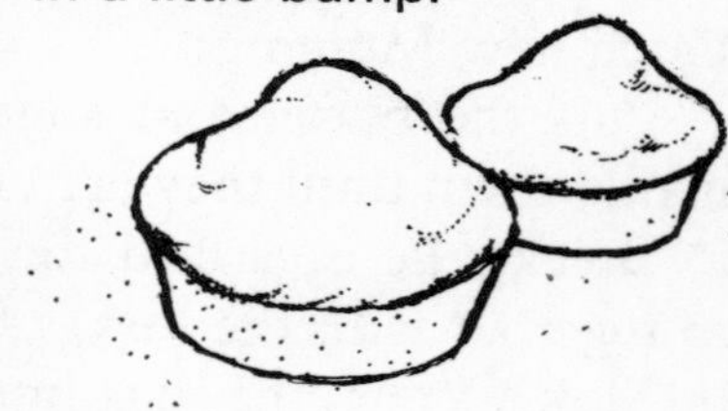

4 When the buns are quite cold, cut a slice from the top of each and then cut the slice in half to make a butterfly.

5 Put a spoonful of butter icing on the bun and place the butterfly on the top with its wings sticking up.

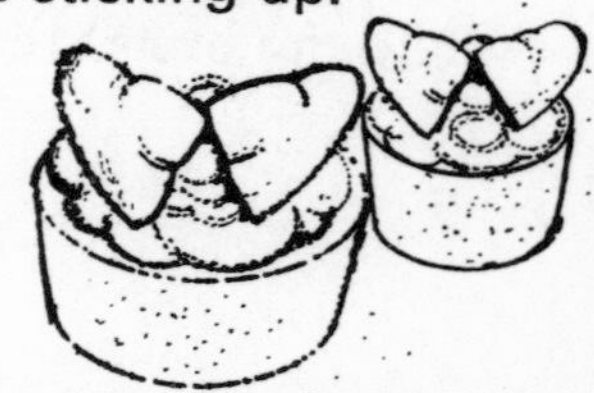

You can help Mummy by picking out potatoes all the same size to scrub. You can help her to dry them and prick them with a fork and put them in a baking tin. Make sure the potatoes do not touch, otherwise they will not bake evenly. If you are going to eat them on a plate and not in your hands at a picnic out of doors, then put a little blob of fat on each to make the skin soft before Mummy puts them in a hot oven (Mark 7, 425°) for about an hour.

Potato boats

FOOD	TOOLS
4 baked potatoes	Knife
¼ lb. cheese	Board
2 oz. butter	Fork
¼ cupful of milk	Plate
Salt and pepper	Grater

1 While the potatoes are cooking cut two thin square slices off the cheese and cut them in half, corner to corner to make four sails for the boats. Grate the rest of the cheese.

2 When Mummy takes the potatoes out of the oven let them cool a little and cut them in half lengthways.

3 Scoop out the soft potato on to the plate and mash it in with the grated cheese, the milk, butter, salt and pepper.

4 Divide this mixture into four and put it back in the shells. Plant a triangle of cheese for a sail in each one.

Next time Mummy makes a stew, ask her to cook some extra vegetables so that you can make Russian Salad to eat with cold meat.

FOOD
1 cupful of cooked carrots
1 cupful of cooked potatoes
1 cupful of cooked turnips and parsnips
1 cupful of cooked onions
A sprig of parsley from the garden
$\frac{1}{2}$ a cup of Salad Dressing

TOOLS
Knife
Board
Bowl

Use the knife with both hands on top of it so you don't cut your fingers. Cut the vegetables up into little cubes, smaller than sugar lumps. Cut the parsley up even smaller. Put salad dressing in the bowl with the vegetables and mix half the parsley with it. Sprinkle the rest on the top.

FOOD	TOOLS
½ lb. cooked fish	Knife
½ lb. cooked potatoes	Fork
1 oz. butter	Board
1 egg	2 plates
1 sprig of parsley from the garden	Greaseproof paper
½ a cup of dried breadcrumbs	Bowl
Salt and pepper	

1 Chop the parsley with both hands, one on the knife handle and one on the top of the knife blade. This chops the parsley smaller and keeps your fingers safely out of the way of the knife.

2 Put the potatoes on one plate and mash them up with the fork. Add the fish and mash it up too. Add the butter, parsley, salt and pepper. Mix them all together.

3 Turn the mixture out on to the board and make it into a roll with your hands like a big sausage. Cut off rounds with the knife.

4 Break the egg into the bowl and mix it up. Put the breadcrumbs on the other plate.

5 Take each round in turn and dip it first in the egg and then in the breadcrumbs so that they stick all over it.

6 You can roll each one through the breadcrumbs like a wheel. Shake off the loose crumbs.

The fish cakes are ready for Mummy to fry in hot fat till they are golden brown.

4 · *A wet day on your own*

Here are some things a Brownie can make all by herself if her mother is busy. Nothing needs heating. The stuffed tomato pots are made out of food that has already been cooked.

Ask Mummy if you can get everything out yourself, wash it up after you have finished, and then surprise her by leaving the kitchen as tidy as a new pin!

FOOD	TOOLS
4 tomatoes about the same size	Knife
1 hard-boiled egg	Fork
1 big cooked potato	Bowl
1 tablespoon cooked peas	Board
1 tablespoon salad dressing	Plate
Salt and pepper	

1 Carefully cut the top off each tomato and scoop out the pulp into a bowl so that you have four empty little pots with four empty lids.

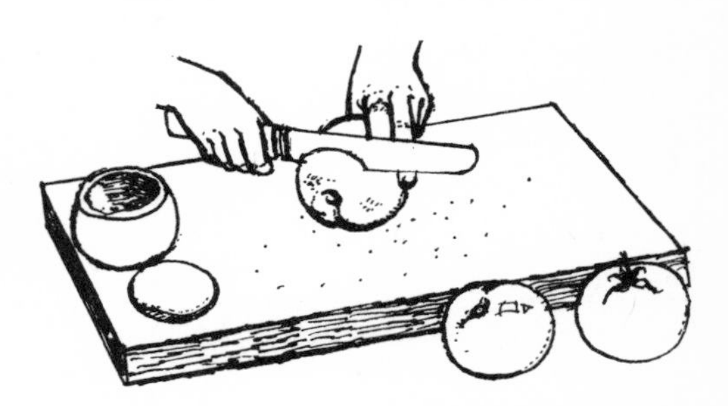

2 Mash the potato and the hard-boiled egg on the plate and mix them in with the tomato pulp, salad dressing, salt and pepper. Stir the peas in last.

3 Fill each pot with this mixture, and pop the lids on.

Quick lottie is a fast relation of apple charlotte (which is made of cooked apples and breadcrumbs baked in the oven). To make one for Mummy and you:

FOOD	TOOLS
2 good fresh apples	Grater
1 cupful of cornflakes	Bowl
2 tablespoons sugar	Lemon squeezer
1 orange	Rolling pin
	Board

1 Crush the cornflakes with a rolling pin on the board.

2 Grate the apple, all except the core. You have to be careful when you grate apple (or cheese) not to grate your fingers too.

3 Hold the apple with your fingers on the outside of it, away from the holes with the sharp little edges that the apple is rubbed up and down on to grate it. Tap the grater so the gratings fall down inside.

4 Mix the apple and cornflake crumbs together and add the sugar.

5 Squeeze the orange by cutting it in half and turning each half round on the lemon squeezer. Pour it over the rest.

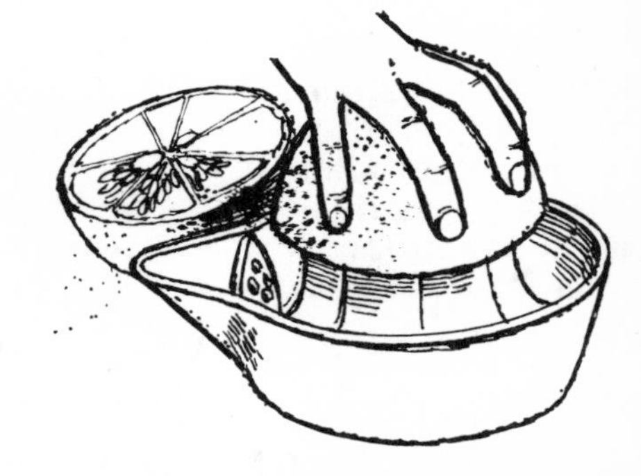

This has to be made very quickly and your hands must be extra clean.

FOOD
1 ready-made Swiss roll
1 family block of ice cream
1 small packet halved almonds
or other nuts
3 currants

TOOLS
Bowl
Plate

1 Take the Swiss roll out of its paper and squidge it into a ball with your hands —this is a very nice feeling and it does not matter if the air gets out.

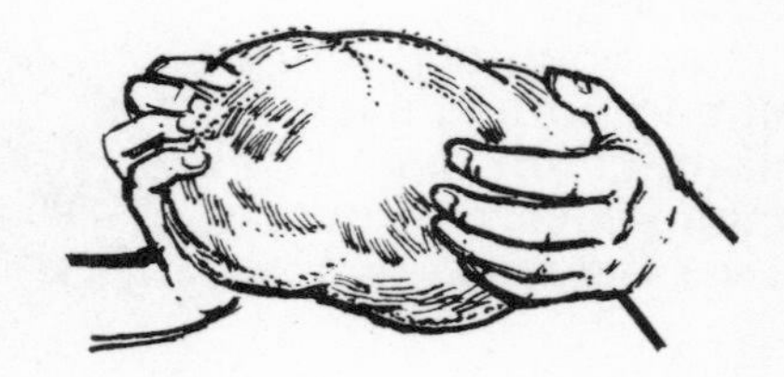

2 Put the ice cream in a bowl and add the squidged Swiss roll. This part will feel rather cold because now you have to squidge the ice cream into the Swiss roll. Never mind if it melts a bit at this stage.

3 Form it into the shape of a hedgehog and stick the nuts in all over it leaning slightly backwards to look like prickles. Put the currants in for eyes and a snuffily nose. Put it back in the coldest part of the fridge till you need it.

Have two bowls ready, one for the white and one for the yolk.

Pick up the egg and tap its side on the edge of one bowl. Then, holding it over the bowl, put both thumbs in the crack and very slowly open the egg up with your thumbs as though it were a book. Let the see-through white—but not the yolk—run out into the bowl through the hinges, while you very carefully tip the yolk into one half of the egg shell, and then pour it back and forth from one half of the eggshell to the other till all the white has run into the bowl. Then put the yolk into the other bowl. Don't let any of the yellow mix up with the white or it won't whisk properly.

You use the white for meringues and making icing sugar stiff. Yolks can be added to scrambled eggs.

FOOD	TOOLS
1 lb. icing sugar	Sieve, Bowl
1 egg white	Knife, Wooden spoon
1 teaspoon lemon juice	Board, Plate
4 drops peppermint essence	Small pastry cutter
	Skewer

1 Sieve the icing sugar into the bowl and add the egg white and lemon juice and mix it up.

2 Dip the skewer into the peppermint essence three times, each time flicking a drop of peppermint into the mixture.

3 Stir well. Put on the board, and knead it with your hands. Flatten it out with your fingers, which may need washing again, or the peppermints may come out grey!

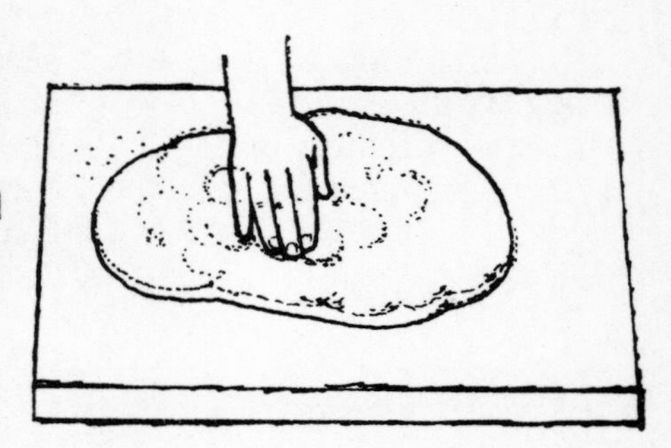

4 Stamp out rounds with the pastry cutter. Any bits left over can be rolled up and pressed out again. Leave the peppermint creams for half an hour or more to go crisp.

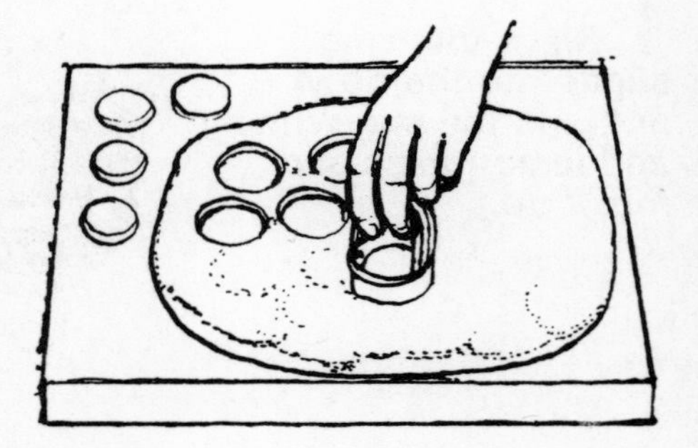

5 · *With Mummy's help*

With her mother's help a Brownie can do a lot of cooking that's useful as well as fun. Some days she could help to choose and cook the supper.

Cheese is very useful for supper but it's not very good for young children or old people at night-time if it's cooked. Just melt it, otherwise even you might get bad dreams.

The best way to melt it quickly is to grate it first. You can use up the hard old bits for grating. This may be harder work but makes a better job of it.

If you want grated cheese to turn a rich gold under the grill or in the oven, mix toasted breadcrumbs with it.

French people often like to eat their bread and cheese in their soup. This makes a nice warming dish on a cold day.

Put a slice of bread in the bottom of a soup bowl, pour the soup over the bread and sprinkle grated cheese over the top. Put the whole bowl under the grill till the cheese on the top has browned crisply and the underneath pieces of cheese have melted and spiralled down to soak into the bread.

FOOD	TOOLS
2 pieces bread	Cheese grater
2 oz. butter	Board
2 oz. cheese	Knife
2 oz. fat	Frying pan
Salt and pepper	Slice

1 Grate the cheese. Spread butter on one side of each piece of bread.

Pile the cheese on the buttery side of one piece.

2 Sprinkle it with salt and pepper. Put the other piece over it, buttered side down to make a cheese sandwich.

3 Cut off the crusts and cut the sandwich into four strips.

Ask Mummy to heat the fat in the frying pan and fry the dreams on both sides until they are golden brown and the melting cheese is just beginning to run out at the sides.

Eat very hot, only not at bedtime unless you want to have Cheese Nightmares!

FOOD	TOOLS
6 oz. flour	Baking sheet
4 oz. butter	Sieve
2 oz. caster sugar	Bowl
Pinch of salt	Rolling pin
Tablespoon of sugar	Wire rack
	Wooden spoon, Fork

1 Grease the baking sheet with the butter paper.

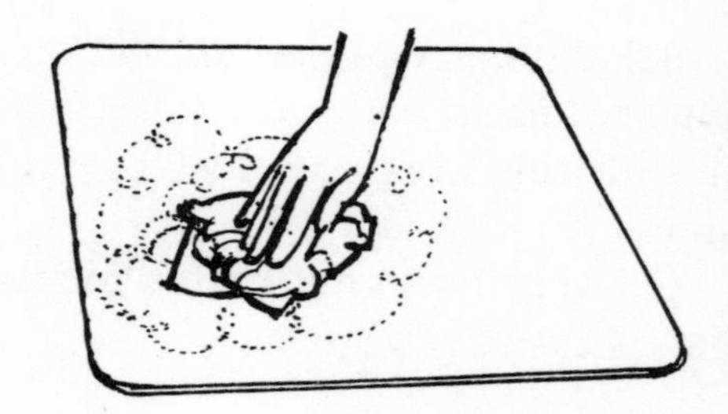

2 Sieve the flour and salt into the bowl and then rub little blobs of the butter into the flour until the mixture looks like bread crumbs.

3 Mix in the sugar and knead it into a ball with your hands.

Roll it out till it is about half an inch thick and put it down onto the baking sheet.

4 Prick it all over with a fork and push up the border with your thumbs.

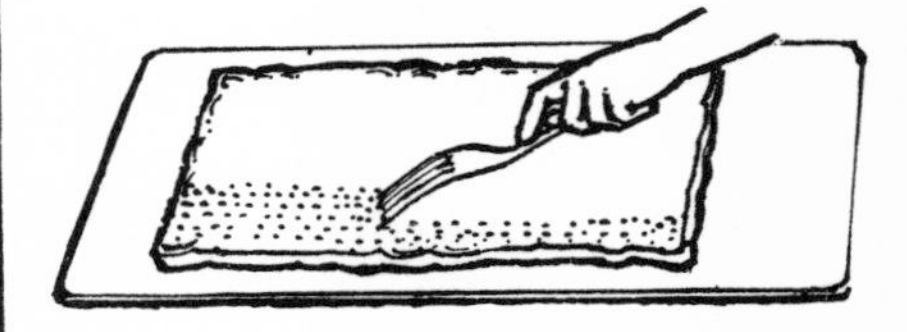

Ask Mummy to put it in a cool oven (Mark 3, 325°) for about an hour. When it's ready, sprinkle the spoonful of sugar over it, cut it up and leave it to get cold on the wire rack.

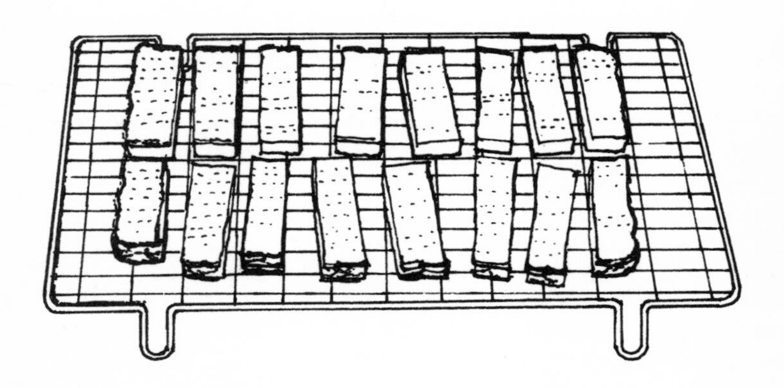

French children call this 'lost bread' because the stale bread would otherwise be thrown away—and so lost.

FOOD	TOOLS
2 slices of stale bread	Bowl
1 egg	Fork
$\frac{1}{4}$ cupful milk	Frying pan
2 oz. butter	Slice
Salt and pepper	Plate

1 Break the egg into a cup and beat it up with the milk. Add salt and pepper.

2 'Let the bread drink the egg and milk,' French children say —'drink' means soak it up.

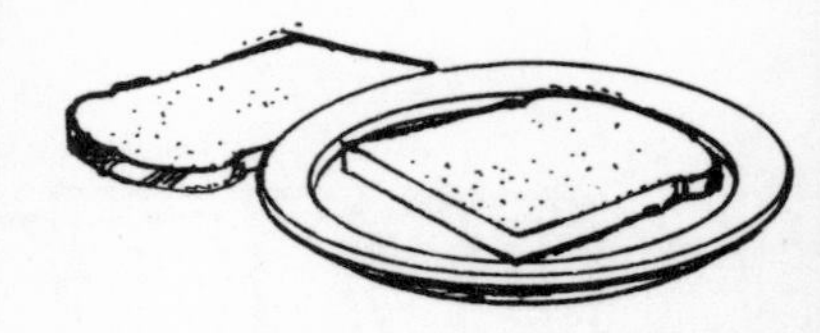

3 Ask Mummy to melt the butter in the frying pan and when it's hot put the lost bread into it and fry it golden brown on one side. Turn it over and fry the other side.

FOOD	TOOLS
½ lb. flour	Cardboard, Knife
2 oz. brown sugar	Scissors, Pencil
2 tablespoons golden syrup	Tracing paper
3 oz. butter	Bowl, Board
1½ teaspoonful of ground ginger	Wooden spoon
½ teaspoon of bicarbonate of soda	Saucepan, Sieve
A handful of currants	Baking sheet
A little water	Wire tray
	Rolling pin

1 Trace this Ginger Nut man. Hold the tracing against the cardboard and cut him out in cardboard while Mummy melts together the treacle and butter in the saucepan and stirs in the bicarbonate of soda.

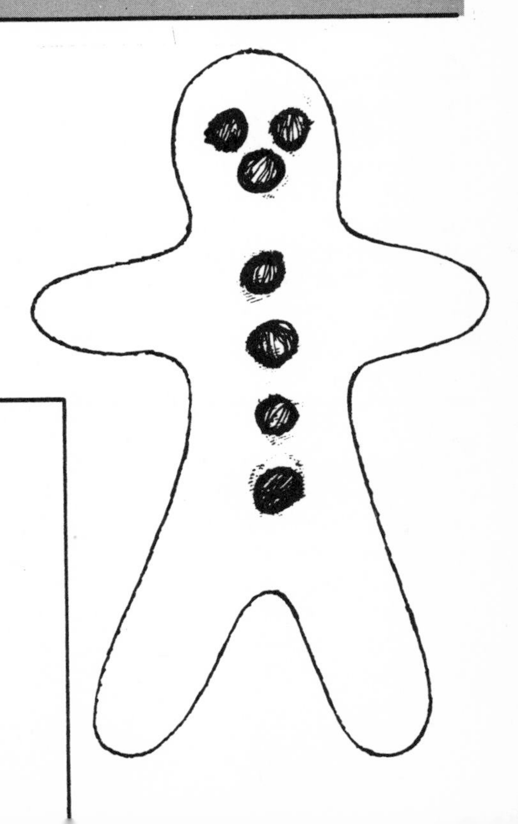

2 Sieve the flour and ginger together through the sieve into the bowl and stir in the sugar.

3 When Mummy has poured the mixture out of the saucepan into the bowl, stir it and mix it to a stiff dough with your fingers, adding a little water if it is too dry.

4 Put the dough on the board and roll till it is as thick as your middle finger. Place the cardboard man on the dough and cut round the shape to make the first ginger nut man.

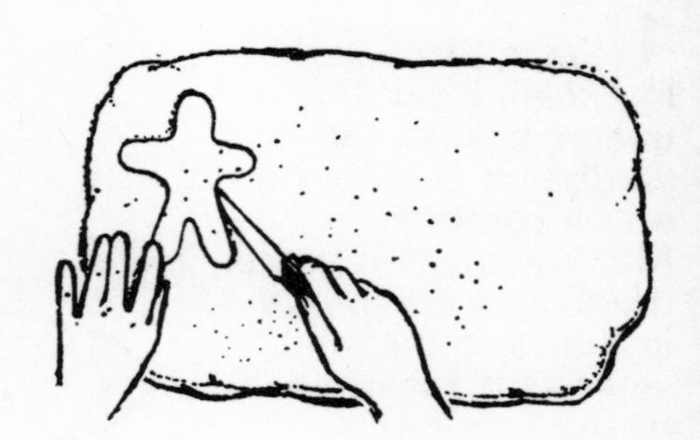

5 Put currants for eyes, nose and mouth on each man's face and down his front for buttons.

6 Rub the baking sheet with buttery paper and arrange the ginger nut men on it but not touching. Mummy will bake them in the oven (Mark 3, 325°) for twenty minutes.

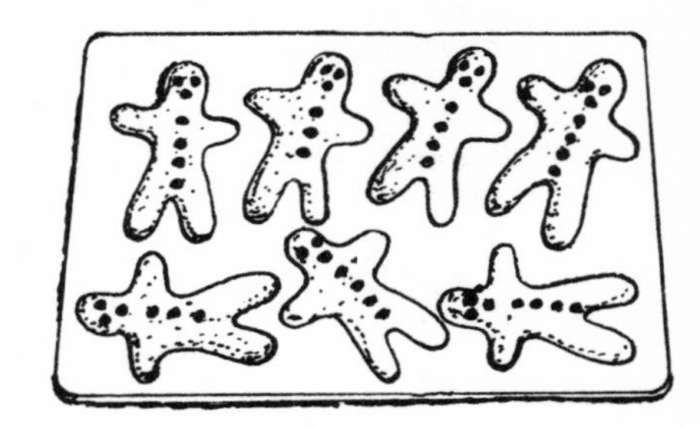

7 When the ginger nut men are done let them cool for a little on the baking sheet and then gently lift them out to get quite cold on the wire tray.

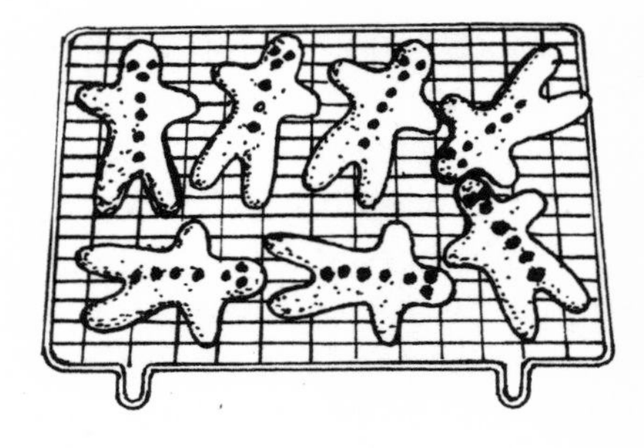

6 · *Look out!*

As you get better and better at cooking so you will have to be all the more careful in the kitchen.

Cooking can be quite dangerous for anyone who is careless. But so is climbing trees or riding a bicycle or tobogganning in the snow. Anything that is exciting has its dangers, and cooking has its own special ones.

Here are some of the awful things that could happen to a Brownie in the kitchen. She could:

1 Burn herself on the hot-plate, pans or the oven door.

2 Scald herself from spilling boiling water or boiling fat or getting in the way of very hot steam (sensible Brownies turn saucepan and frying pan handles inwards so they don't knock against them, making sure that handles are not over hot-plates).

If you get burnt or scalded put the hurt part in cold water at once and SHOUT for help.

3 Cut herself with a sharp knife or when opening a tin or turning an egg whisk fast with her fingers in the way or putting her fingers too close to the grater when she's grating cheese.

If you cut your finger, hold it under the cold tap till it stops bleeding. Keep it CLEAN. Put a clean plaster dressing on.

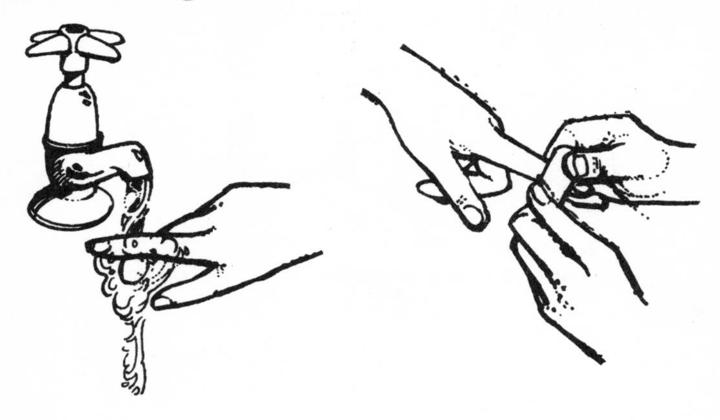

4 Get an electric shock from pulling out a plug without first switching it off, or from touching electrical things with wet fingers.

If it's a small shock, you'll soon jump out of the way. If it is a bad one and it happens to somebody else, switch off the electricity before touching the person. YELL FOR HELP.

5 Set the frying pan on fire.

Switch off the heat.

Don't throw water on. Don't try to carry the flaming pan out. Put a big lid, or a bigger saucepan, or a floor mat over the frying pan to shut all the air out from the flames. SCREAM FOR HELP.

6 Set herself on fire.

Roll on the floor, if possible in a rug or coat. If it's someone else on fire, make them do the same. SHRIEK FOR HELP.

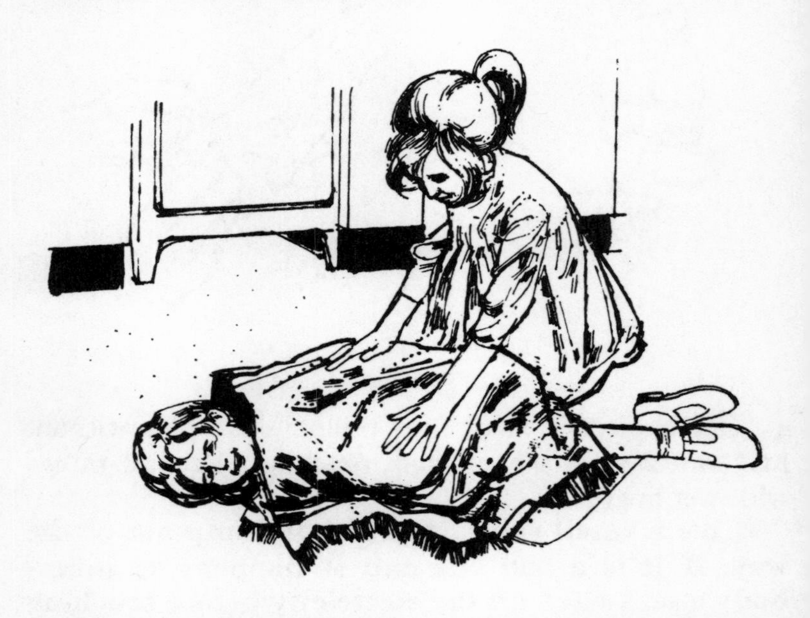

Can you think of any other terrible things that could happen to a careless Brownie in the kitchen?

Just to remind you—NO Brownies boil or bake or fry or roast without a grown-up there to say they can!

7 · *Easter and other egg surprises*

Which do you like best? Getting a surprise or giving a surprise? Do you like to come down to breakfast on Easter morning and find brightly coloured hard-boiled eggs piled up in the middle of the table? Or do you like to be the one who paints them the day before and gives everybody else a surprise?

For hundreds of years people have changed the colour of egg shells for Easter Day, wrapping them in coloured cloth with colours in it that ran, or with spinach to make them green. Nowadays most people have paint boxes so it's more fun to paint the hard-boiled egg in the patterns you want. You can paint faces on them and then make little paper hats.

If you like giving surprises you could collect empty egg shells and wash them out and put a little yellow woolly chicken and a tiny present in one for Mummy and another for Daddy and put them upside down in their egg cups. When they crack them on Easter morning what a surprise! Or you could fill the empty egg shells up with chocolate.

FOOD (for 2 eggs)
4 oz. milk chocolate
1 pint water

TOOLS
Bowl
Saucepan
Wooden spoon
2 empty egg shells

1 Put the bowl in the saucepan and pour the water round it. Break the chocolate up into the bowl and put the saucepan on to heat.

2 Stand the empty egg shells in egg cups, openings uppermost. Stir the chocolate to make sure all the lumps have gone, and when it is melted spoon it into the empty egg shells and leave it to harden in a cool place.

3 For cream-filled eggs, make round peppermint creams and pop them into the egg shells when they are only half filled with the melted chocolate.

4 Fill up with the rest of the chocolate. 4 oz. of chocolate will make three cream-filled eggs.

5 Leave the shells on for surprise or peel them off if you want to show the eggs are really chocolate.

Eggs

One exciting thing about cooking is the way the same kind of food behaves differently according to the way you cook it.

Eggs are especially surprising. FRY AN EGG in a little fat and you can see the white changing from sloppy see-through jelly with a round orange yolk sliding about in it, to a firm white-bordered daisy with a flat orange centre. The moment it does this, slide the slice under it and lift it quickly but gently onto a plate. (If it goes on cooking any longer, the underneath will grow into a tough leathery skin and the yolk will go harsh and dry.)

Odd things happen to a POACHED EGG (which you break into a saucepan of shallow boiling water instead of into a frying pan full of fat). If you don't trap the egg at the beginning with a pastry cutter or special poacher a lot of loose bits of cotton-woolly looking white will start tearing about the saucepan.

BAKED EGGS behave rather like fried eggs, except that you can't watch them all the time because they are cooked in the oven. Rub each ramikin pot with buttery paper and break an egg into each one. Put them in the oven for about seven minutes (Mark 4, 350°). Leave them a bit longer if they have not quite set.

With a BOILED EGG the surprise doesn't come till you open it. Have you cooked it too long or too short? Is it hard as an india rubber or liquid as a drink of orange juice? Three and a half minutes by the clock or an egg timer, in water that is already boiling, is long enough to boil a soft egg that has been in the kitchen for a day or in the larder for a week. If the egg comes straight out of the fridge or has been laid only that day it needs a minute longer.

HARD-BOILED EGGS need at least five minutes boiling to be on the safe side. Some people prefer to eat their breakfast eggs hard. Cold hard-boiled eggs are very useful for picnics or to go into salads or chopped up in sauce to eat with fish.

As soon as hard-boiled eggs come out of the saucepan they need to go into cold water to make them easy to peel. It also stops them going grey round the yolk.

You might think that scrambled eggs and omelettes are the same. You need eggs, butter and salt and pepper for both but the way you cook them makes all the difference.

FOOD
2 eggs
1 oz. butter
1 tablespoonful milk
Salt and pepper

TOOLS
Saucepan
Bowl
Wooden spoon
Fork

1 Break the eggs into the bowl, whisk with the fork and add the milk, salt and pepper.

2 Gently melt the butter and pour the mixture in. Keep stirring until it thickens.

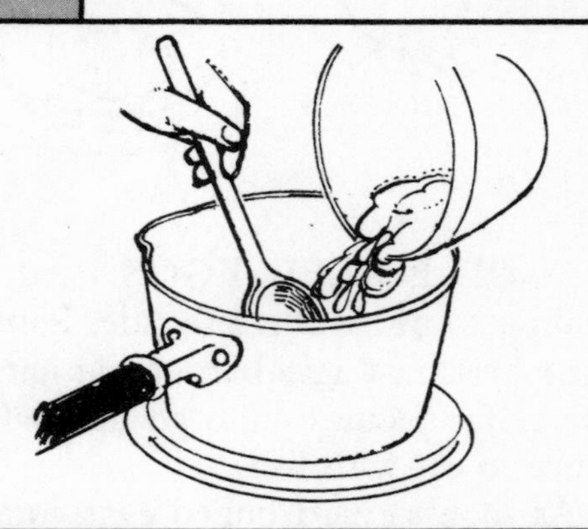

Scrambled eggs need to cook very slowly and not too long. They will go on cooking a little bit after you take them off the heat, so allow for this.

Scrambled eggs on toast that has been buttered are very good for supper.

FOOD
2 eggs
½ oz. butter
2 tablespoonfuls water
Salt and pepper

TOOLS
Frying pan
Bowl
Fork
Slice

1 Break the eggs into the bowl and whisk with the fork. Add the water, salt and pepper.

2 Melt the butter in the frying pan. Pour in the egg mixture and give one big stir and then leave it for a minute until it sets. That's the difference from scrambled eggs!

Omelettes need cooking very quickly, scrambled eggs slowly.

You can put some grated cheese in the omelette or some chopped-up ham or cooked mushrooms. Fold the omelette in half and it is ready to eat.

Add flour to eggs and butter and milk or water and all sorts of other different things happen, according to how you cook exactly the same mixture. It's the cooking that counts! ! Did you know that pancakes and Yorkshire Pudding are exactly the same mixture? Only pancakes are *fried* and Yorkshire pudding is *baked*.

For BATTER for BOTH you need:

FOOD
4 oz. flour
1 egg
$\frac{1}{2}$ pint milk
(or milk and water)
1 oz. butter or fat
A pinch of salt

TOOLS
Bowl, Sieve,
Wooden spoon

1 Sieve the flour and salt into the bowl, then make a hollow in the centre and break the eggs into the hollow.

2 Gradually stir the flour into the egg, adding a little milk as you go. Keep on beating until all the milk is used up.

For pancakes you will also need a frying pan and slice.

1 Melt the butter in the frying pan to cover the bottom and push some round on to the sides.

2 When the fat is smoking hot, pour in a little batter, just covering the bottom of the pan. Cook the pancake until it is golden brown on the bottom and then turn it over and cook the other side. Some people toss them over.

Sprinkle a little sugar on each and a squeeze of lemon and roll it up and keep it warm while you cook the next one.

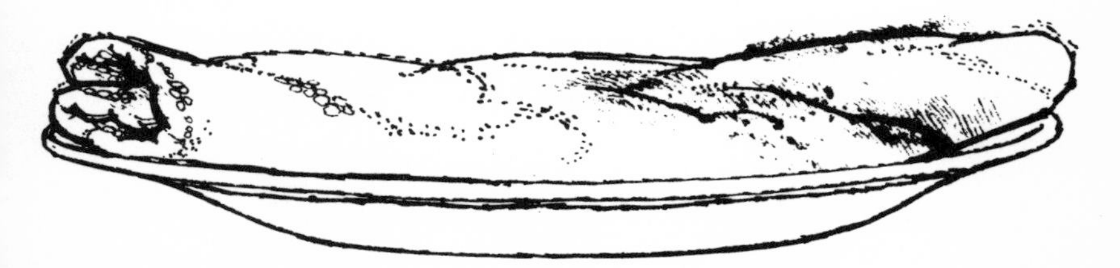

For Yorkshire pudding you will need a baking tin instead of a frying pan and slice.

1 Put the butter or fat into the baking tin and melt it in a very hot oven (Mark 9, 475°). When it's smoking hot take the tin out and pour the batter into it.

2 Bake for half an hour. See how it rises, opening and shutting the oven door very gently. When you take it out and cut it up it tastes and looks completely different from pancakes!

Egg points

Broken eggs pick up smells from other foods, so cover them up and use them as quickly as possible.

Put eggs in the larder with the pointed side downwards. They keep fresher that way.

When you break eggs into a cake or batter, break them first one by one into a cup in case one is bad.

For people who like their fried eggs turned, just gently turn the egg over and cook it again upside down for a few seconds only.

You can keep pancakes for two or three days in a cool place and then warm them up when you need them.

8 · *Cook to a golden brown*

What happens if you add sugar to the flour and milk and butter needed to make pancakes and Yorkshire pudding? If you mixed it up in a different way and boiled it in a basin you would have a sponge pudding. Bake the same mixture in the oven and you will have a cake, or put it in patty pans and you have a batch of buns.

There are hundreds of kinds of puddings and cakes and buns that all come out differently because of the way you cook them and the little extras you put in at the beginning, like cherries or sultanas or chocolate or nuts.

With Yorkshire pudding and pancakes you put the floury, eggy, milky mixture into the fat, which is already sizzling hot. With cakes you mix the fat into the flour and sugar first.

There are two ways of doing this. You can mix the fat with the sugar until it is all creamy. This is called creaming the fat. It's best for rich cakes, with a lot of fat in them.

Or you can rub the fat into the flour with the tips of your fingers. This is called rubbing the fat in. It's best for plain cakes.

FOOD	TOOLS
8 oz. flour	2 Bowls
3 oz. butter	Wooden spoon
1 egg	Fork
2 oz. sugar	Sieve
The grated rind of a lemon	Wire rack
A little milk to mix	Patty pan tin
Pinch of salt	Skewer

1 Cream the fat and sugar till pale and soft.

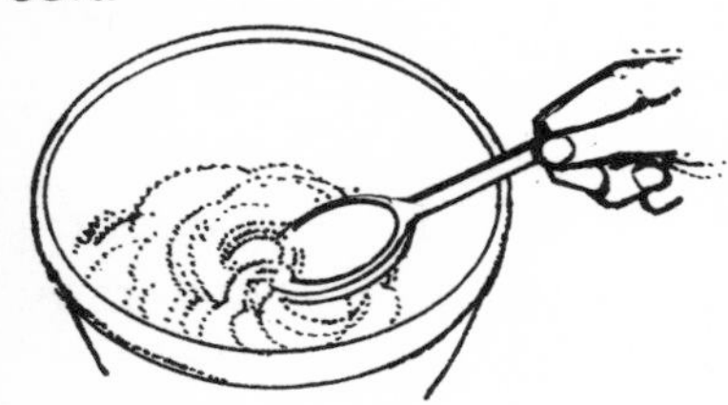

2 Break the egg into a basin and whisk with the fork. Pour it gradually into the creamed sugar and butter, keeping it smooth and creamy.

3 Sift the flour and salt through the sieve to let in more air. Let the flour fall first on the outside and then gradually stir it into the middle with a few drops of milk. Stir in the grated lemon rind.

4 Put spoonfuls of the mixture into the patty pan tins leaving room for the buns to swell.

Bake for about fifteen minutes in the middle of a medium oven (Mark 5, 375°).

Test with a skewer to see if they are done.

Don't open the door and let the cold air in at the beginning or the buns will fall flat.

When you take them out let them wait for a little while in the tin before you turn it upside down on the cooling rack.

If you want to make a cake instead of buns, line a cake tin with kitchen paper by drawing round the tin on to the paper and cutting it out to fit the bottom of the tin. Put more paper round the sides. Rub both sides of the paper with butter.

Pour all the cake mixture into the tin and give it a tap to get the air bubbles out. Pile up more at the sides than in the middle because the middle will rise most.

A cake will take a bit longer to cook than buns so you need not test it so soon.

When it is done leave it in the tin for a few minutes before you turn it upside down on the cooling rack. Don't cut the cake till it is quite cold.

Cake points

Make sure the flour is dry and the eggs and milk and butter are fresh. Some people think that food that is not fresh enough to be eaten by itself can be tossed into a cake. So it can be, but the taste is just as horrid inside the cake as out. Don't put in too much flavouring, it makes the cake soggy.

Heat the oven and get the cake tins ready before you start cooking. Make sure you have the right size. If the tin is too big the cake will come out too flat—if too deep it may not cook in the middle at all.

Rich cakes with a lot of fat in them may burn unless you line their tins with kitchen paper greased on both sides. Sift in a little flour.

Fill the tin two-thirds full and then gently bang it to make sure air bubbles come out. You want to keep the air in but not in great bubbles that leave holes when the cake is cooked.

Steamed pudding

If you want a pudding for lunch you make exactly the same mixture but instead of putting it into patty pans and baking it in the oven you get a small basin and rub the inside with butter paper and put the mixture in this instead.

1 Cover it with a saucer upside down and put the bowl in a saucepan half-full of water. Boil the saucepan with the lid on for about an hour.

2 Take the basin out with a cloth, take the saucer off and put a plate upside down over it. Turn the bowl upside down on to the plate and there is your pudding. You can eat it with golden syrup or jam.

FOOD	TOOLS
8 oz. flour	Bowl
3 oz. butter	Sieve
4 oz. sugar	Wooden spoon
Half a cup of milk	Board
Jam: raspberry or apricot	Baking sheet
Pinch of salt	Wire rack
	Knife

1 Rub the baking sheet with buttery paper.

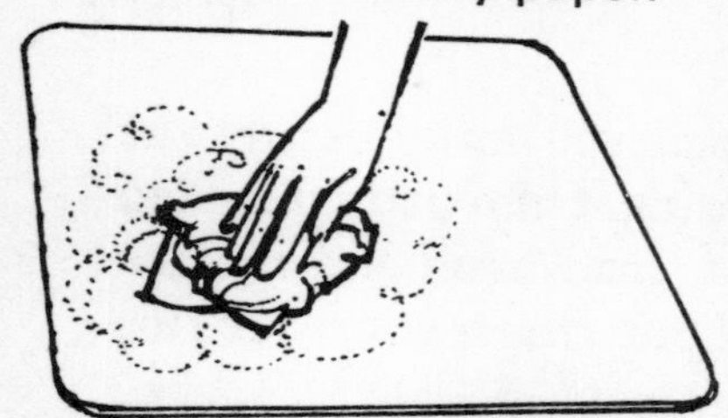

2 Sift the flour and salt into the bowl and rub little blobs of the fat into the flour with the tips of your fingers till they turn into fine crumbs.

3 Add the sugar and enough milk to mix it to a stiff dough.

4 Turn on to a board and knead lightly. Divide into little pieces about the size of an egg.

Make a hole in each and put some jam in it.

5 Put on the baking sheet and bake in a hot oven for about twenty minutes. (Mark 7, 425°).

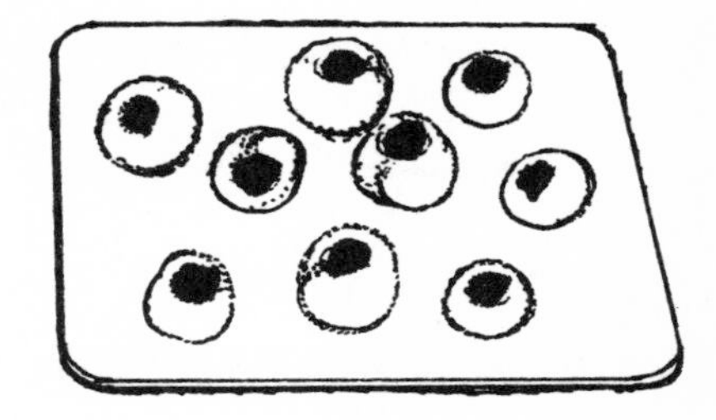

9 · *White cooking and red*

Cooking flour and butter and milk without eggs mostly comes out white. Cook flour and butter and milk in a saucepan and you have white sauce. Bake it in the oven and you have scones and pastry. (Don't bother to try frying it; nothing comes out worth eating.)

"Once you can make white sauce you can make anything," some people say.

FOOD
1 oz. butter
1 oz. plain flour
½ pint of milk
½ a chicken stock cube
Pepper

TOOLS
Saucepan
Wooden spoon, Jug

1 Melt the butter in a saucepan over a low heat.

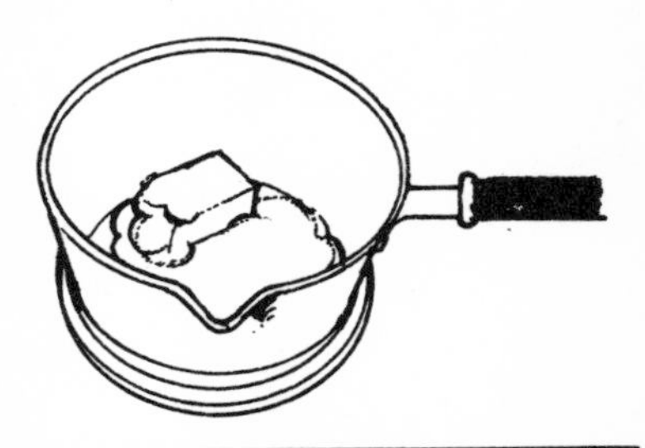

2 Stir in the flour and keep stirring for three minutes.

3 Remove from the heat and add a little of the milk.

4 Put back on low heat and add milk little by little, stirring all the time. Once you feel the spoon gliding over the bottom of the pan you can add the rest of the milk more quickly.

5 Add the crumbled chicken stock cube and pepper and bring to the boil, stirring all the time. Cook gently for at least five minutes.

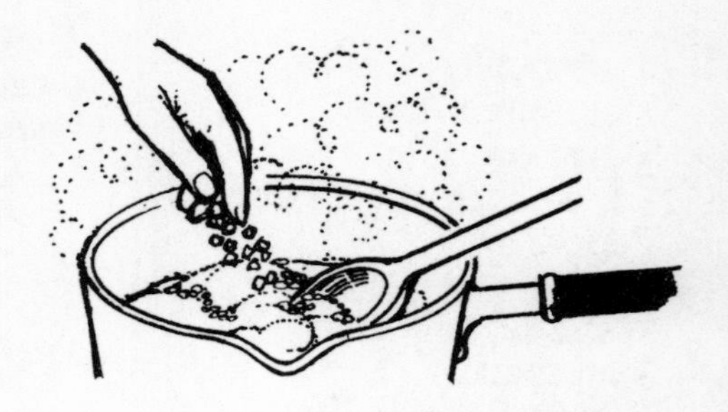

Use a wooden spoon. A metal spoon gets too hot. Find a wooden spoon you like that fits your hand and isn't too heavy or too short. Make that your favourite. Once you have learned to make white sauce you can do all sorts of exciting things with it. You can add grated cheese or chopped hard-boiled egg or a small tin of salmon.

Once you can make pastry, too, then you're getting to be Quite a Cook!

This is the most useful kind to make for jam tarts, treacle tart and rhubarb pie.

FOOD
8 oz. flour
6 oz. butter
Water to mix
Pinch of salt

TOOLS
Bowl, Knife
Sieve, Board
Rolling pin

1 Sieve the flour and salt and stir in the fat cut into pieces.

2 Mix in enough water to make a stiff dough. Knead it, to get the air in. But don't squash it.

3 Put on a lightly floured board and roll out into a long strip, keeping the edges straight by patting them in.

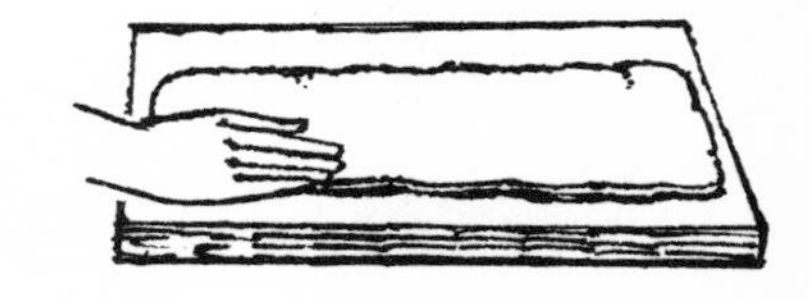

4 Fold the pastry into three. Roll lightly and fold again ; keep folding and rolling three or four times over. Then leave for a little while.

Now you can turn it into any kind of tart or pie you like.

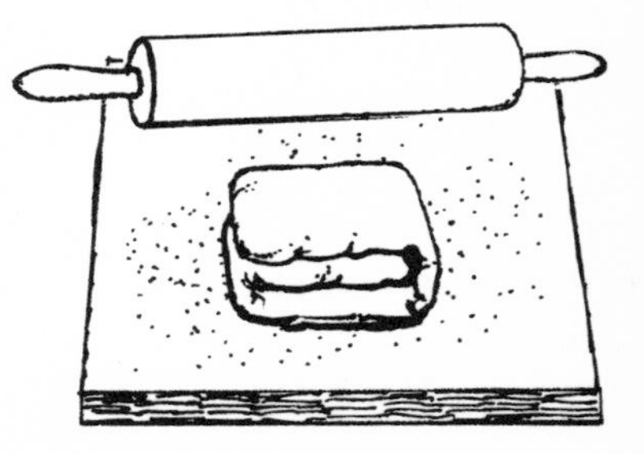

FOOD
About 5 sticks rhubarb
4 tablespoonfuls of sugar
½ a cup of water
Pastry

EXTRA TOOLS
Pie dish
Egg cup
Fork

1 Wash the rhubarb and cut it up into lengths about an inch long. Throw away the leaves and the white bottom of each stalk. They are poisonous.

2 Roll the pastry out thin and put the pie dish on it upside down and cut round the edge of it, but not too close as the pastry may shrink. Cut strips and a few leaves from the left over pastry.

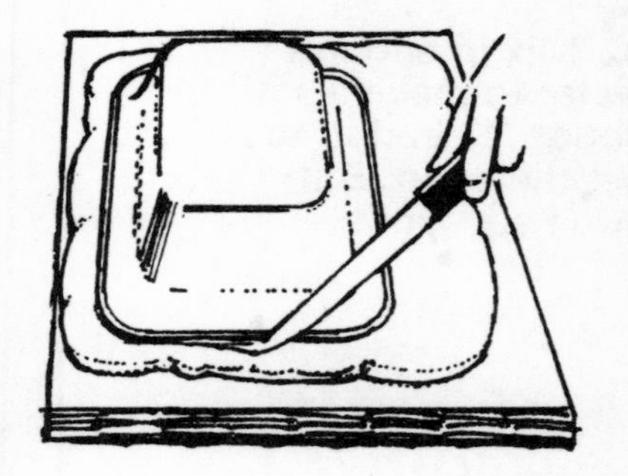

3 Put the egg cup upside down in the middle of the pie dish and pile the rhubarb up round it. Sprinkle the sugar on and add the water.

4 Wet the rim of the pie dish with your finger and lay the strips round it. Wet the strips with your finger and put the pastry lid on to the pie dish and go all round the edge with a fork making a pattern.

5 Make a little hole in the middle to let the steam out and arrange the leaves round the hole. Bake in hot oven for half an hour. (Mark 8, 450°.)

FOOD
4 tablespoonfuls golden syrup
4 tablespoonfuls breadcrumbs
Pastry
Flour

EXTRA TOOLS
Flan tin

1 Roll the pastry out thin and put the flan tin on it upside down. Cut round it, a little bigger than the actual flan tin.

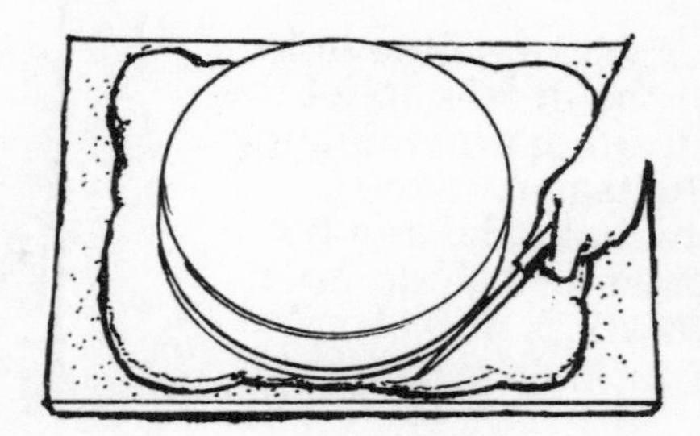

2 Lightly flour the flan tin and put the pastry round on it. Press it down in the middle and spread the crumbs on it up to about an inch from the edge.

3 Twiddle spoon as you pour the treacle on the crumbs. Never mind if it's all in one place. When it melts it will spread out.

4 Cut the pastry scraps into thin strips and twist each one like barley sugar. Lay the twists across the crumbs and syrup in a criss-cross pattern. Bake in a hot oven for 20 minutes. (Mark 8, 450°.)

Pastry can be used in all sorts of exciting different ways. What other ways can you think of?

If you like you can make the pastry one day and keep it in a cool place till the next day before you roll it out and bake it.

Jam tarts

FOOD
Slice of bread
Jam
Pastry
Flour

EXTRA TOOLS
Pastry cutter
Patty pans
Wire rack

1 Heat the oven to Mark 8 (450°) and lightly sprinkle the patty pans with flour.

2 Roll the pastry out again and stamp out rounds with the pastry cutter. Put a round in each patty pan and press it down a little.

3 Break the bread up into pieces about as big as a lump of sugar and put a piece of bread in each round to stop the pastry rising up in the middle.

4 Put the tin in the oven for about ten to fifteen minutes and when the tarts are done, take them out and throw away the toasted bread Let the tarts cool on the wire rack and then put a spoonful of jam in each.

The faster scones are made, baked and eaten, the better they will be. Making scones is a good way of using up sour milk.

FOOD
8 oz. flour
2 oz. butter
$\frac{1}{2}$ cup of milk
Pinch of salt

TOOLS
Bowl, Metal spoon
Board, Rolling pin
Pastry cutter
Baking sheet

1 Sift the flour and salt into the bowl.
Rub the butter in with your fingers, breaking it up and squidging it into the flour with the tips of your fingers.

2 Make a well in the centre with a metal spoon and pour in *fast* (not slowly as for batter and white sauce) enough milk to make a light spongy dough when you stir it.

3 Turn on to a floured board and knead very lightly. Roll out one inch thick.

4 Dip the cutter into flour and stamp out rounds. Be gentle and quick, patting them into shape as quickly as you can.

Put the scones on a floured baking sheet and bake for about ten minutes in a hot oven. (Mark 8, 450°.)

5 Don't split the scones with a knife, before they are buttered, but with your fingers.

Most food changes a bit once you cook it. It may change in colour or get softer or harder. It may swell up or rise up, but one thing you may be sure, it will always taste nicer and be better for you if it's cooked the right way.

Uncooked rice would be very hard to eat, however hungry you were! See what happens when you cook it.

If you are in a hurry you can cook rice instead of potatoes, which need peeling.

FOOD
$\frac{1}{2}$ lb. rice
2 pints water
1 tablespoonful salt

TOOLS
Big saucepan
Colander

1 Almost fill the saucepan with the water and put the salt in.

2 When the water is boiling furiously drop all the rice in. Cook for twenty minutes.

3 Strain through the colander and turn the cold tap on to it to wash away the starch.

4 Put the colander of rice over the saucepan which you have refilled with water and let it steam till you need it.

FOOD
Two lamb chops
1 tablespoonful fat
Salt and pepper

TOOLS
Frying pan
Slice
Tinfoil
Roasting tin

Watch what happens to red meat when you cook it.

Fry the chops in the hot fat for one minute and then turn them over. You will see how the outside has changed colour and gone brown and hard. This is fine because the new hard shell will keep all the good juices inside. If the chop went on cooking very fast for long, all the meat inside would be hard and not very nice. To make sure it will be really good and tender finish cooking them slowly in the oven. Put the chops side by side on the tinfoil. Sprinkle with a very little salt and pepper and fold the sides of the tinfoil over to make a parcel.

Don't make a very tight parcel of it. Leave plenty of room for the nice warm air inside.

Ask Mummy to put it in the oven at Mark 5 (375°) for about half an hour.

Unwrap the chops at the table, one for you and one for Mummy. When you cut yours, it should be a nice pinky brown inside and dark brown outside.

Can you think of other food that changes in different ways when you cook it?

Look through this book for ideas, and other cook books too.

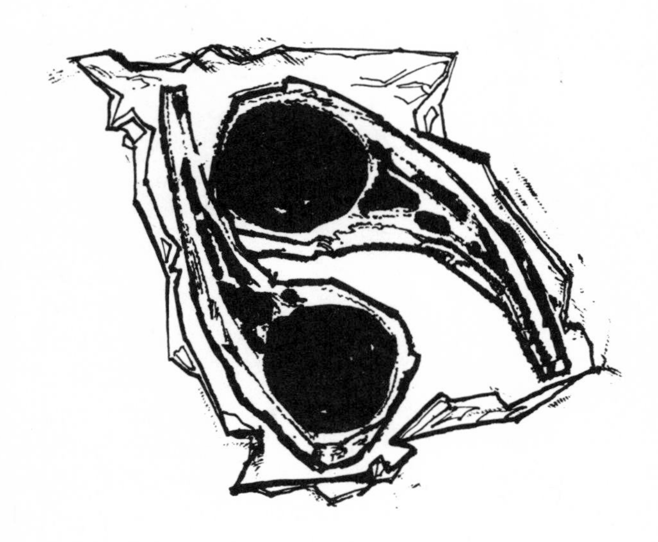

10 · *The picnic basket*

There are two ways of getting a picnic basket ready. One is to tear round looking for any leftovers, put them all in paper bags and hope for the best.

The other way is to plan the picnic the day before and make one or two things specially for it. And then on the day make the sandwiches and drinks.

But maybe you don't know you're going for a picnic till an hour or so before. Even then there will be time to make scones or rolls.

FOOD
1 lb flour
3 oz. butter
$\frac{1}{4}$ pint of milk
1 teaspoonful of salt

TOOLS
Board, Wooden spoon
Bowl, Baking sheet
Pastry cutter

1 Rub the baking sheet with buttery paper.

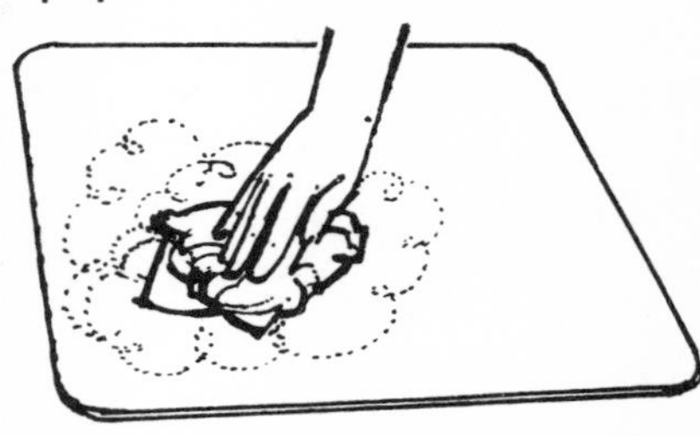

2 Rub the fat into the flour and add the salt and milk to make a soft dough.

3 Cut and shape into small rounds and put on the baking sheet.

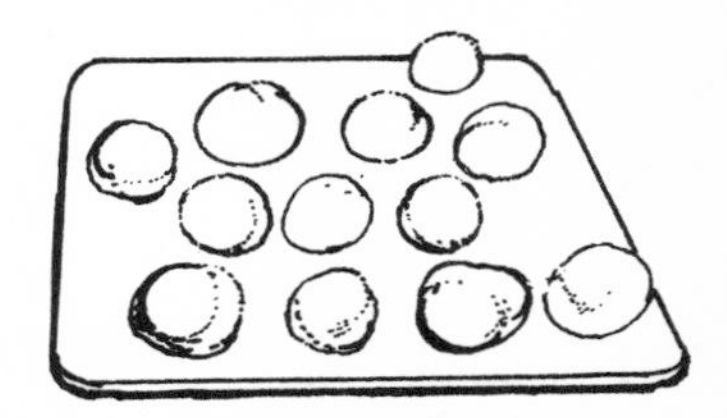

4 Bake for ten minutes in a hot oven. (Mark 8, 450°.)

FOOD
4 oz. butter
4 oz. soft brown sugar
8 oz. porridge oats
2 tablespoons golden syrup
Pinch of salt

TOOLS
Saucepan, Wooden spoon
Square baking tin

1 Rub the baking tin all over with buttery paper.

2 Melt the sugar, butter and golden syrup slowly in a saucepan. Add the porridge oats, mixing all the time. Stir them all together.

3 Put the mixture in the baking tin and cook in a medium oven for twenty minutes. (Mark 4, 350°.)

When cool cut into squares.

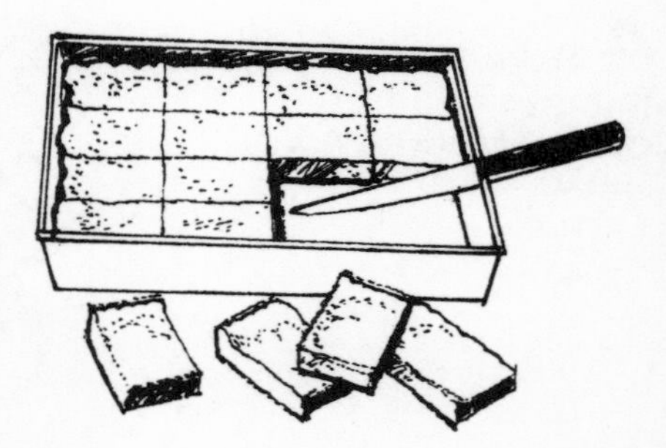

The honey sandwiches for Teddy's tea party would be good for a picnic, only make them bigger. You could also make them of lemon curd or potted meat or Marmite. Jam and marmalade are not so good as they soak through the bread and make you sticky.

Leave the butter in the kitchen for a little while to make it soft. Don't try to melt it in a saucepan.

When you spread it on the bread keep the knife flat so that the butter stays smooth on the top of the bread and isn't dug into it so that the taste and feel of butter is lost.

Leave the crusts on for lunch sandwiches.

For double-deckers use three slices of bread for each sandwich. Butter the middle slice on both sides and put different fillings on each deck.

Try grated apples and sultanas on the upper deck, banana below.

Cheese and dates above, cheese and tomatoes below.

Cottage cheese and pineapple above, ham below.

Cream cheese and watercress above, nuts below.

Useful things to take on a picnic are hard-boiled eggs, cold sausages, apples, bananas, or any food that can be eaten in the hand.

Useful drinks are orangeade, lemonade, or tea or coffee in a thermos. If you take a thermos rinse it out first with hot, not boiling, water before you pour the tea in.

Pour it right up to the top even if you don't expect to drink it all. It keeps hotter that way. Don't add the milk to tea but take it separately in a little bottle.

You can add the milk to coffee in the thermos. Don't forget the sugar, and take unbreakable cups or mugs. If it's a cold day take soup in a thermos. Thick soup is all right if you take spoons to eat it out of the mugs with.

Tomatoes and lettuce are useful. Wash the lettuce well before you start, and put it for about ten minutes in the bottom of the fridge to get crisp.

Polythene bags are better than paper ones because you can see what's inside them.

Don't forget a cloth and paper napkins.

For hard-boiled eggs take salt done up in little twists of paper.

Crisps and peanuts are useful, but don't give peanuts to babies and small children. They may choke.

11 · *Mummy's day in bed*

What happens if you have a bad cold? You stay in bed and Mummy brings you your meals on a tray. Maybe you don't feel very hungry but she makes everything look so good you eat a little after all and feel much better.

What happens if Mummy has a bad cold? If there's nobody to look after her she has to get up and feel awful. So why not give her a day in bed too? She will feel better much more quickly if you take her tray very nicely laid with light food that is easy to eat.

Here are some things to remember when you are looking after ill people.

Start making the meal early to make sure it is ready at the usual time or even earlier. Time passes slowly in bed and late meals don't seem to taste so good.

Lay the tray very carefully with a spotlessly clean cloth, shining knife and fork and spoon and a polished glass. Choose small plates and only put a little food on each. Cover food up to keep it warm, but make sure lids fit so they don't slide off going upstairs.

Surprises help to make the time pass in bed, and though you can ask Mummy what she would like, put a little surprise on the tray as well. It could be a small bunch of flowers in a shallow vase or it could be a special little surprise dish. She will have quite a surprise anyway when she sees you come in with the tray. But let her eat her meal quietly.

Take the tray away as soon as she has done and make her comfy. Leave her books and papers and a glass of water near her, then leave her in peace for a rest.

If she really feels dreadfully weak give her a straw for her drink so she does not have to sit up to drink it.

Making tea

1 Fill the kettle with fresh water from the tap.

2 Put the kettle on the heat and wait for it to boil.

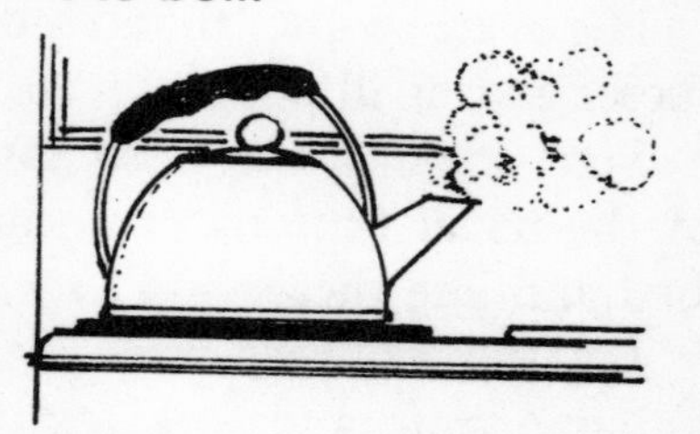

3 Pour some boiling water into the teapot and swill it round and pour it away. This is to warm the pot.

4 Put in one teaspoonful of tea for each person and one for the pot.

5 Make sure the kettle really is boiling and then put the teapot near it and pour the boiling water over the tea leaves.

6 Always take the teapot to the kettle and not the kettle to the teapot and make sure there are no children underneath it who might get scalded.

7 Cover with a tea cosy and allow to stand for 3 to 4 minutes before pouring out.

If you have a small teapot that is not too heavy to carry upstairs, make Mummy's tea specially for her in this.

If not, pour it out downstairs and add the milk and sugar if she likes it and take it up all ready for her to drink.

1 Boil the kettle.
Put a teaspoonful
of Bovril in a cup.

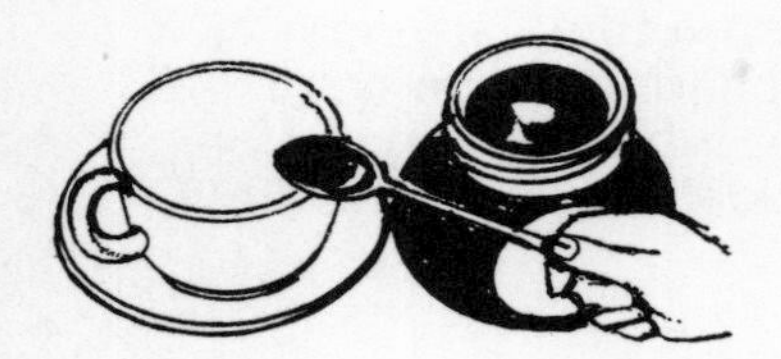

2 Pour boiling water
over the Bovril,
stirring all the time.
Put salt and pepper
on the tray in case
Mummy wants it.

3 Light the grill or
switch on the toaster.
Put a slice of
bread on the grill or
in the toaster.
Watch it carefully.

4 When it is golden
brown take it out. Don't
leave it lying flat or
it will go soggy. Cut the
crusts off and cut it in
half, corner to corner.

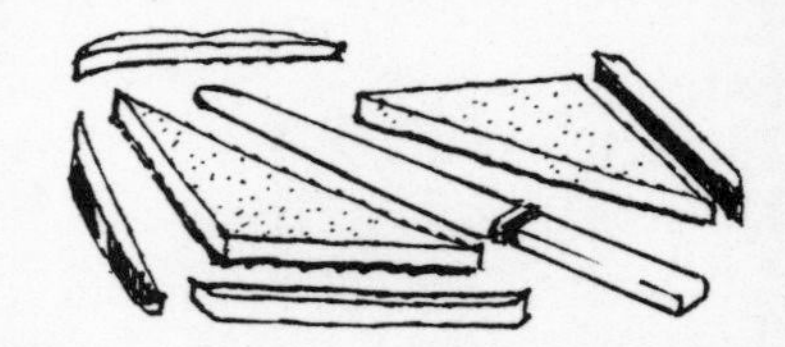

5 Put the two triangles
of toast in a toast
rack.

This is very good
for people who have
been sick.

Lay a tray for breakfast with:

Clean cloth
Cup and saucer and teaspoon
Small side plate
Egg cup on a saucer
Knife, Egg spoon
Salt and pepper
Little jug of milk
Little dish of butter
Little bowl of honey or marmalade
Teapot on a mat with tea cosy
Shallow vase of flowers
Toast rack
Table napkin—very important in bed

Practise walking upstairs with the tray with a few unbreakable things on it so you can learn to hold it level, so cups and saucers and plates don't slide about.

A good warm comfort after having a tooth out.

FOOD
$\frac{1}{2}$ pint milk
1 slice of bread
1 tablespoon sugar

TOOLS
Saucepan
Wooden spoon
Porridge bowl

1 Remove the crusts and cut the bread into squares.

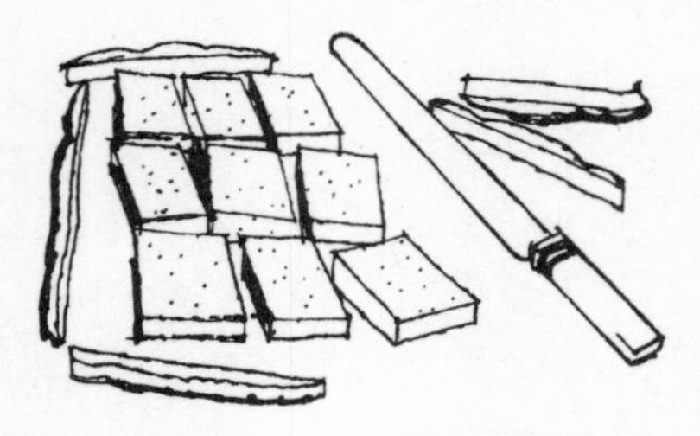

2 Put it in the bowl and sprinkle it with sugar.

3 Warm the milk but do not let it boil.

4 Pour the hot milk over the bread and cover it up while you carry it upstairs.

This is very good for colds and coughs.

FOOD
3 onions
½ pint milk
Salt and pepper
½ chicken cube
½ pint water

TOOLS
Knife
Board
Saucepan

1 Cut the onions up very finely and put into the saucepan with the milk and ½ pint of water. Add the salt and half chicken cube.

2 Cook very slowly until the onion is soft. Stir in the rest of the milk and pour into a bowl.

3 Serve it with a slice of bread and butter.

FOOD
3 lemons
3 tablespoons caster sugar
2 tablespoons honey
$1\frac{1}{2}$ pints water

TOOLS
Lemon squeezer
Knife
2 jugs
Sieve
Spoon
Kettle

1 Squeeze the lemons and then cut the peel up as small as you like.

2 Put the lemon juice and cut-up peel in a jug with the sugar and leave it while you boil the kettle.

3 Pour on a pint and a half of boiling water and stir in the honey.

4 Strain into another jug and pour out into a glass with a spoon in it to stop it breaking.

Good after a tummy upset.

Ask Mummy if you can go out and buy some nice fresh fish for her lunch. Tell your fishmonger what you want it for and ask him to pick you out a really good fish and fillet it for you. That means cut four neat slices off the bone, two each side. Mummy will only need two fillets, so buy the other two for yourself if you like fish.

FOOD	TOOLS
4 small fillets of plaice or sole	2 plates
Salt	Saucepan
Juice of ½ lemon	
2 oz. butter	
1 pint water	

1 Half fill the saucepan with water and put one plate on the top.

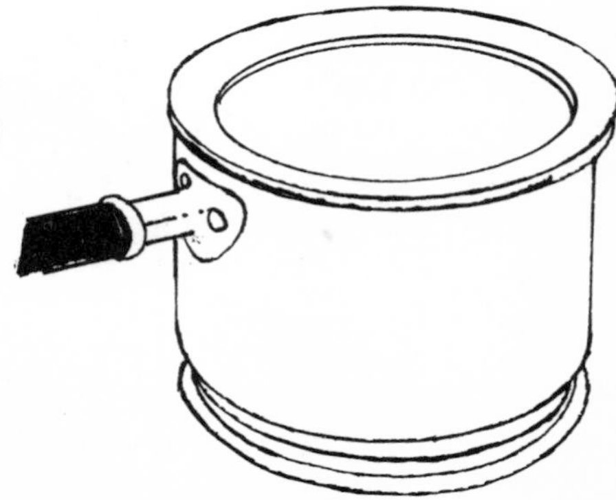

2 Lay the fillets on the plate and squeeze the lemon on to them and sprinkle with salt.

3 Put the saucepan on the hot-plate, with the second plate upside down over the fish, like a lid.

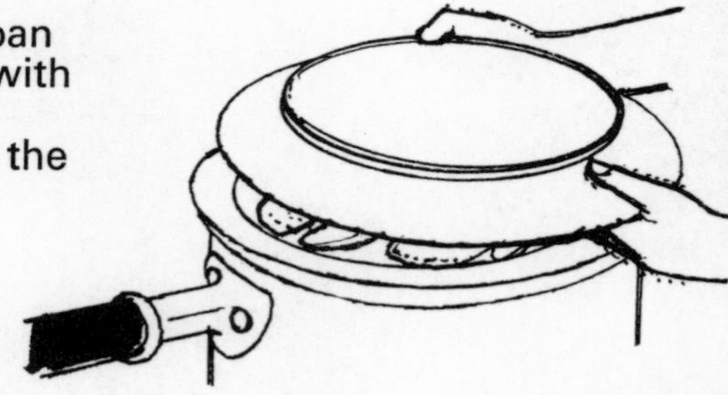

4 Turn on the heat. Start timing the fish as soon as you hear the water bubbling. Turn off the heat after five minutes.

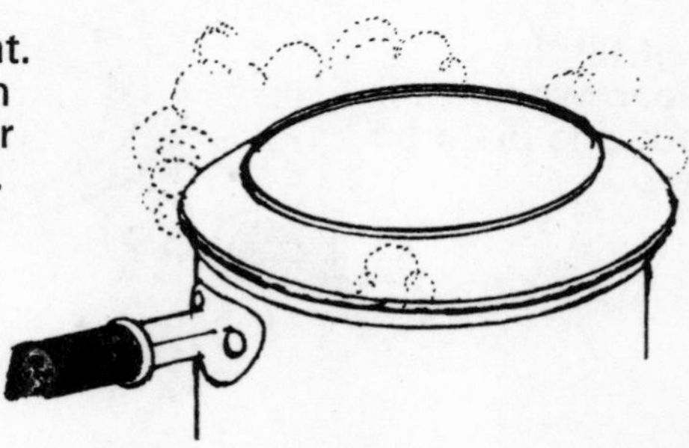

5 Wearing gloves, carefully lift off the top plate and turn it the right way up. Then lift off the underneath plate.

6 Gently lift your two fillets on to the top plate. Put a blob of butter on each fillet and take Mummy's up to her while it's still piping hot.

FOOD
1 orange
2 tablespoons sugar

TOOLS
Scissors
Bowl
Board

1 Cut the orange into a basket shape as in the picture.

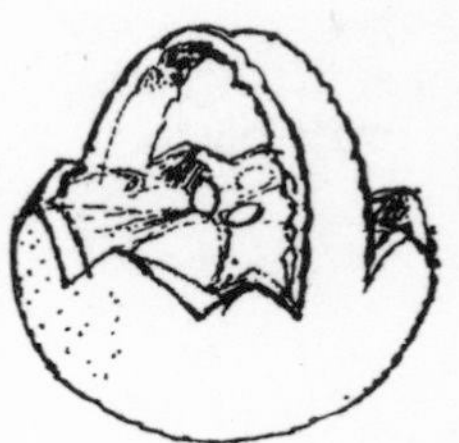

2 Take out all the fruit, cut it up small and throw away the pith.

3 Pour all the sugar over it and leave it to soak it up.

4 Put the fruit back into the basket. Don't forget to put a spoon on the tray for it.

This is enough for Mummy and you too. You may have to go out and get the ice creams.

FOOD
2 single ice creams
$\frac{1}{4}$ lb. sugar
1 tablespoon milk
1 oz. butter

TOOLS
Saucepan
Wooden spoon

1 Melt the sugar in the milk and very slowly bring it to the boil. Add the butter little by little and boil it for five minutes stirring all the time.

2 Keep it warm but not still cooking while you put an ice cream in each bowl.

Pour the hot fudge over each ice cream and eat at once.

FOOD	TOOLS
3 eggs	Kitchen paper
4 oz. caster sugar	2 tablespoons (metal)
½ teaspoonful olive oil	Baking sheet
	Wire tray
	Egg whisk

1 First dip two fingers in the oil and rub them all over the kitchen paper and spread it on the baking sheet.

2 Separate the eggs into yolks and whites and put the yolks aside in a cup for scrambled eggs another time.

3 Whisk the whites with the egg whisk until they stand up stiffly in peaks.

4 Add half the sugar to the egg whites and beat them up again.

5 Fold in the rest of the sugar very gently with the spoon so the air doesn't escape.

6 Wet the spoons and spoon the mixture on to the paper in little heaps like half eggs.

7 Put them in the middle of the oven (Mark $\frac{3}{4}$, 275°) for two hours till they dry out.

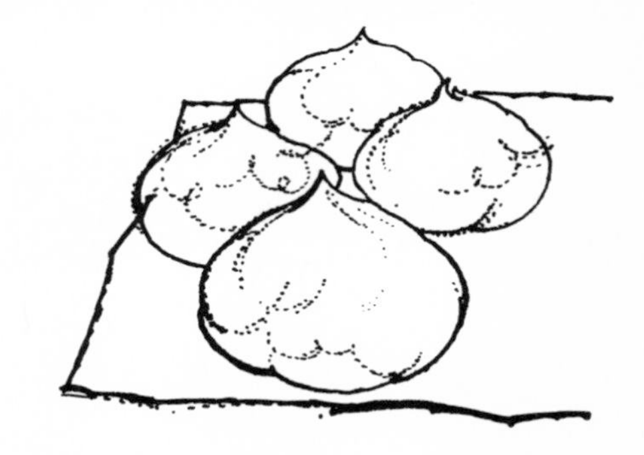

12 · *A cook-and-bring party*

Why not have a Brownie cook-and-bring party? For party cooking it's best to cook in pairs because party food takes longer to cook than every-day food. Each pair can choose something to make at home. Here is some party food to choose from or you can choose from some cakes and scones and surprises in other parts of the book. Or you can look through other cook books and find something good to make.

Carry the food very carefully so it doesn't spoil on the way. A big biscuit tin is the best thing to take food in if you have a long way to go.

Get ideas for sandwiches from the Picnic Basket, only for a party, cut off the crusts and make them smaller and neater. Use different kinds of bread—brown bread, malt bread, and fruit and nut bread if you can get it. Spread the sandwiches with peanut butter, lemon curd or chocolate spread. Try out unusual mixtures like apricots and walnuts, cranberry sauce and almonds, only taste them first to see if they are nice.

FOOD
2 one-inch thick slices of white bread
2 one-inch thick slices of brown bread
1 pot meat or fish paste
2 oz. butter

TOOLS
Knife
Board

1 Remove the crusts and trim the slices of bread to the same size, spread both brown slices and one white slice with butter and paste.

2 Pile the slices up on the top of each other in alternate colours—brown, white, brown, white.
Press down slightly and slice through the middle.

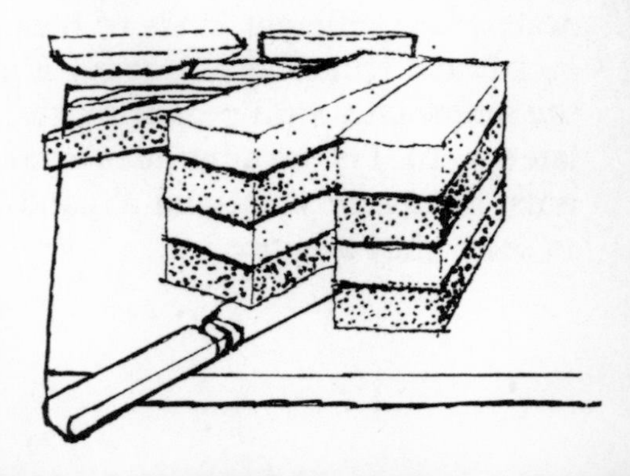

3 Spread butter and meat paste down the side of one pile. Turn the other pile upside down and press piles together again.

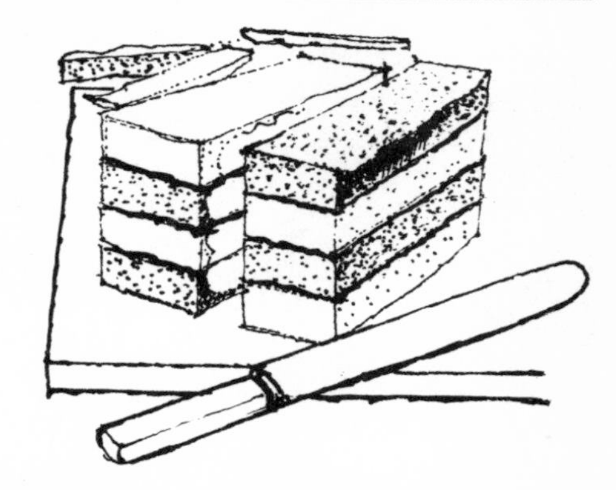

4 Cut this chequered loaf into slices for the party.

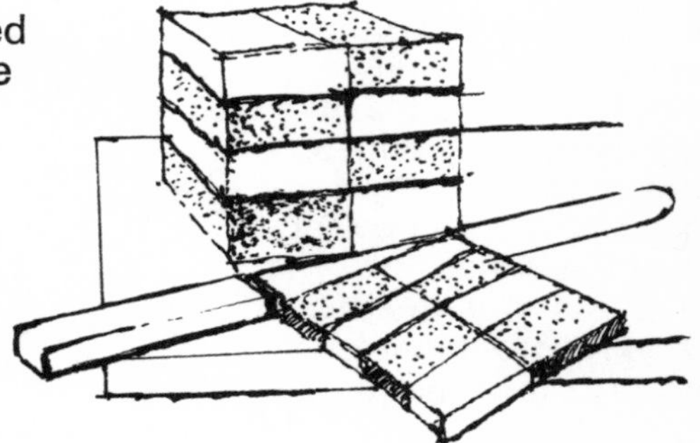

5 Arrange the different kinds of sandwiches on a tray or very big plate with little bits of parsley here and there.

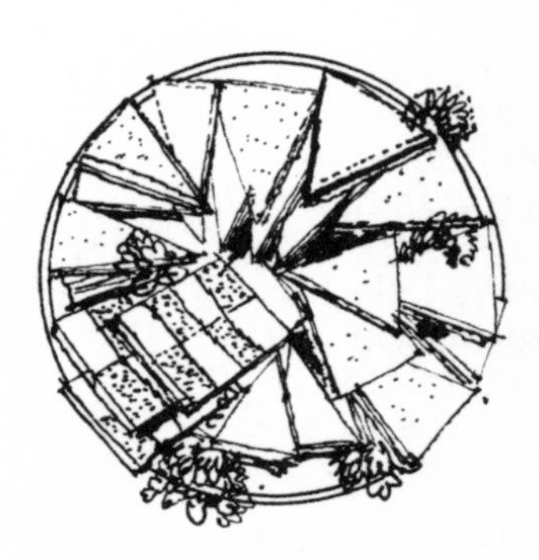

FOOD	TOOLS
2 packets of orange jelly	1 pint measuring jug
3 oranges	Tablespoon
Water	Scissors
	Kettle
	Jelly Mould
	Bowl

1 One Brownie cuts the oranges in half with scissors to make jaggy water lily edges, then scoops out fruit and cuts it up, throwing away the white pith. The other Brownie divides the jelly into squares and puts it in the jug.

2 Boil the water and pour it on the jelly stirring all the time until the jug is half full.

When the jelly has dissolved pour it into the bowl and start again with the other packet.

3 This time rinse out the mould with cold water and put the fruit in the bottom. When you pour the boiling water on to the jelly cubes in the jug, make it come to just under half a pint.

4 Pour the jelly on the fruit in the mould and leave both jellies in a cool place for several hours. Take the jellies to the party in their moulds and when you get there turn them out.

5 For the water lilies spoon the jelly out of one bowl on to the plate and put some into each water lily orange skin.

Turn the other jelly out on to a plate.

Jelly can be quite difficult to set, especially in hot weather. Sometimes it is difficult to dissolve too. To help it along soak the jelly cubes for a few minutes in cold water then top up with the right amount of hot water.

Adding fresh fruit or lemon juice can make it a bit sloppy, so use a little less water than it says on the packet.

Don't pour the jelly into the mould while it is still hot or it may come out cloudy. Wait until it is cool but still runny.

Jelly mustn't go into the fridge until it is cool or everything else in the fridge will get too warm. Never put it right into the freezing part or it will turn into an iced lolly.

When you take it out of the fridge, give it a few minutes to get back its flavour.

To get it out of the mould dip the mould for a moment into very hot water. This is the tricky part. It must be in the hot water long enough, or part of the jelly will stick to the mould, but not too long or the mould will get too hot and the jelly will start to melt before it has come out. Then turn it upside down on a plate and, holding very tight, shake it up and down. Go on shaking even after you hear the glub glub sound that means it has begun to come out.

If it all breaks up, mash it up with a fork and put it in a bowl instead of on a plate.

Jap cakes

FOOD
3 eggs
6 oz. caster sugar
4 oz. ground almonds

TOOLS
Egg whisk, Basin
Baking sheet, Spoon
Kitchen paper
Pastry cutter

FOOD FOR BUTTER ICING
4 oz. butter
8 oz. icing sugar
½ teaspoonful of instant coffee

TOOLS
Bowl
Knife
Spoon

1 Rub the baking sheet with buttery paper. Separate the egg yolks from the whites.

2 Whisk the egg whites until they are very stiff.

3 Fold in half the sugar and mix the rest of the sugar with the ground almonds and fold into the whisked egg whites.

4 Spread on the baking sheet about a quarter of an inch thick and bake in a moderate oven (Mark 4, 350°) for about twenty-five minutes.

5 Meanwhile make the butter icing by mixing the butter and icing sugar together and stirring in the instant coffee.

6 Take the meringue mixture out of the oven and stamp rounds out with a pastry cutter.

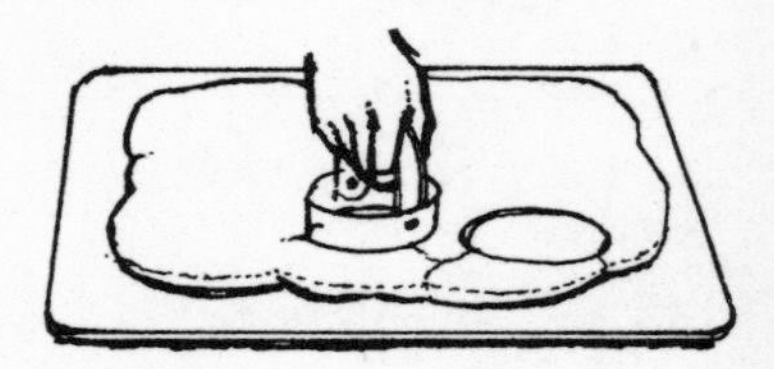

7 Put back in the oven for ten minutes with the trimmings. Take out and crumble the trimmings finely.

8 Spread some butter icing on the top of a round and put another upside down on it. Spread butter icing all over the top and sides of this "sandwich" and dip the top in the crumbs.

9 Roll the cake through the crumbs to cover the sides with them. Scrape crumbs away in the middle and decorate with a blob of butter icing.

FOOD	TOOLS
2 oz. butter	Bowl
4 oz. sugar	Sieve
4 oz. flour	Board
1 egg	Wooden spoon
1 cup of porridge oats	Baking sheet
Cherries to decorate	Wire tray for cooling
	Knife

1 Rub the baking sheet with butter paper.
Cream the butter and sugar and beat in the egg.
Sift the flour through the sieve and stir it in.

2 Wet your hands and make the mixture into balls. Put some porridge oats on the board and roll the balls on it.
Put the balls on the baking sheet and press each one down slightly.

3 Bake in a moderate oven (Mark 4, 350°) for about fifteen minutes.
Let the Melting moments cool slightly on the tray before putting half a cherry on each one.

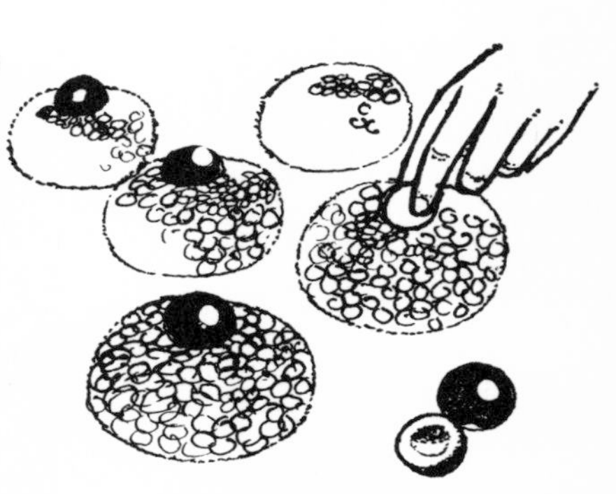

FOOD	TOOLS
1 lb. brown sugar	1 large saucepan, Cup
2 oz. butter	Wooden spoon, Hammer
2 tablespoonfuls vinegar	Chopping board
$\frac{1}{4}$ pint water	Baking tray
1 tablespoon golden syrup	6 Wooden sticks about 6 inches long (you can peel garden sticks but wash them before you use them)
6 really good crunchy apples	

1 Wash the apples under warm running water to get rid of the natural oil. Rinse under cold water, and dry very well.

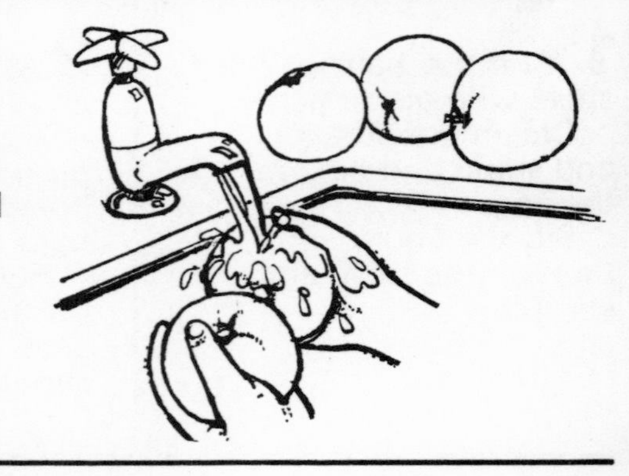

2 Push a stick into each apple beside the stalk and right up through the core. Grease the baking tray with the butter paper.

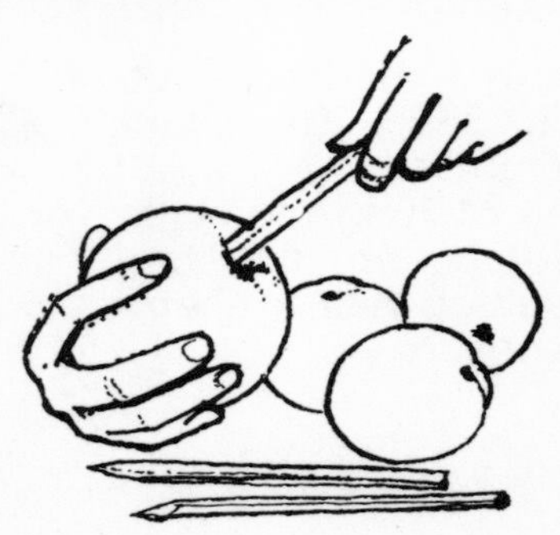

3 Put everything except the apples into the saucepan and heat gently until dissolved. Then boil fast for five minutes, stirring to prevent sticking.

4 Test the syrup by dropping a little into a cup of cold water. If it forms into a hard ball it is ready. If not, go on boiling until it does.

5 Take one apple on a stick at a time and dip it into the toffee and twiddle it round several times, then take it out and let some of the toffee run off it before putting it on to the baking tray to cool.

There is only one thing wrong with toffee apples, and that is that the toffee is not very good for your teeth. After you have eaten any sweets always try to eat an apple to clean them. With toffee apples this is easy enough because if you begin on the outside you are sure to end up with the apple.

FOOD

1 family block of strawberry ice cream
1 small tin of strawberries, or special ready-made syrup for iced drinks
Soda water

TOOLS

Tin opener
6 tall glasses, 6 Spoons, 6 Straws, 1 Tablespoon
Soda water syphon

1 Put a spoonful of ice cream in the bottom of each glass.

2 Open the tin and put two tablespoonfuls of the juice on the ice cream. You can use the strawberries in a trifle.

3 Squirt soda out of the soda syphon into each glass till the froth comes up over the top of the glass.

4 Put a straw and a long spoon in each glass so you can both suck and spoon.

If you want to make other kinds you can use ready-made syrup with different kinds of ice cream.

Lemon syrup goes with vanilla ice.

Chocolate syrup goes with chocolate or vanilla ice.

Raspberry juice with vanilla ice.

Pineapple syrup with vanilla ice.

For the shell:

FOOD	TOOLS
8 oz. flour	Scissors
6 oz. butter	Thin cardboard
Salt and pepper	Sieve, Bowl
2 tablespoons water	Knife, Board
1 tablespoon tomato purée	Rolling pin
	Tracing paper, Pencil

1 Sift the flour, salt and pepper.

Put the butter into the flour and cut it with a sharp knife into small pieces. Rub these into the flour between your fingers and thumb till they are as fine as breadcrumbs.

2 Mix just enough water with the tomato purée to add to the flour and butter to make a smooth pink dough.

3 Roll it out. Fold and roll again to half an inch thickness.

4 Make a tracing of the crab. Hold the tracing against the cardboard and cut it out in cardboard.

---

5 Lay the cardboard crab onto the pastry and cut round it. Claws and pincers can be cut out separately. Bake in a hot oven (Mark 7, 425°) for twenty minutes.

For the Filling:

FOOD	TOOLS
½ lb. tomatoes	Knife
1 hard-boiled egg	Board
1 oz. butter	Saucepan
1 onion, finely chopped	Bowl
1 tablespoon vinegar	Wooden spoon
Salt and pepper	Bowl of hot water
Parsley from your garden to decorate	

1 Put the tomatoes in a bowl of hot water for 5 minutes to peel easily.

Melt the butter in a saucepan till brown, add the tomatoes, chopped onion, and cook until smooth.

2 Chop the hard-boiled egg, and stir it into the mixture for a minute till it thickens.

Pour into a basin and add the pepper, salt and vinegar to taste.

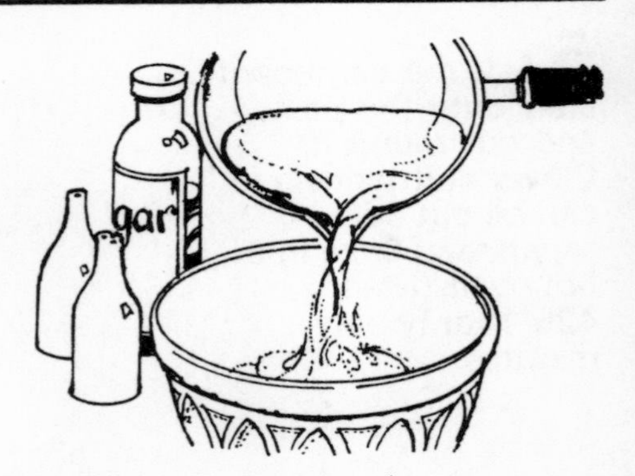

The pastry should rise just enough to form a crab-like case. Separate the top from the bottom with care and scoop out any soft under-cooked pastry from the middle and throw it away. If you eat it it may give you a bad tummy-ache.

Put the filling on to the bottom half of the crab shell and without pressing it down put the top case on to it; arrange the claws and pincers. Decorate it with parsley.

FOOD
8 oz. flour
3 oz. butter
3 oz. sugar
2 oz. currants
2 oz. sultanas
2 eggs
Half a cup of milk
A pinch of salt

TOOLS
2 bowls
Wooden spoon
Sieve
Wire rack
Cake tin

1 Get the cake tin ready with a lining of buttery paper.

Sift the flour and salt into the bowl and rub the fat in with the tips of your fingers and add the sugar.

2 The other Brownie can be washing the fruit and drying it in a cloth. Then dip it for a moment in flour and then shake the flour off. She can beat the eggs in another basin.

3 Stir currants and sultanas into the mixture and then beat in the eggs and milk.

4 Put it into the tin and bake in a moderate oven (Mark 7, 425°) for about an hour.

Leave it to cool for a little and then turn it out very carefully upside down on the rack.

FOOD	TOOLS
½ lb. small sweets – such as dolly mixture	Plate
The right number of candles	Knife
1½ lb. icing sugar	Fork
2 egg whites	Spoon
½ teaspoon lemon juice	Bowl
4 drops of colouring	Jug (of hot water)
1 tablespoon apricot jam	Sieve
	2 cups

1 Put the plate upside down with the cake, still upside down, on it. If it rocks about you will have to cut some of the lumps on the top, now the underneath, off to make it steady.

2 Spread the apricot jam thinly over it to keep the crumbs in place.

The other Brownie can be sieving the icing sugar into the bowl.

3 Then break the eggs and separate the whites from the yolks into the two cups (the yolks can be used to add to something else—like scrambled eggs).

4 Pour the white and the lemon juice into the icing sugar and mix it till it's quite smooth. Add drops of colouring. At first it may seem too stiff. The more you mix it the softer it gets.

5 Put a huge blob of icing on the top of the cake. Dip the knife in the hot water and gently spread the icing all over the top of the cake.

6 Put smaller blobs one by one on the sides and spread with the knife round it. When the knife gets crumby, you can scrape it on the side of the jug and re-dip it in the hot water to make the icing smooth.

When the whole cake is covered up with icing, both Brownies can make patterns on it with the little sweets —and candles.

The cake will take about a day to harden. Carry it to the party on another plate in a big, shallow cardboard box, or on a tray.

Index